Endorsement

"In *A Picture and a Thousand Words*, Kellie offers a gentle yet profound invitation to slow down and see life through a sacred lens. In a culture obsessed with image, applause, and endless comparison, she points us back to what is eternal — to gratitude, grace, and the quiet beauty of a life anchored in God. With tender honesty, Kellie writes about the struggles we all face — worry, aging, disappointment, and the fear of not feeling good enough — and reminds us that transformation begins when we let go of the world's narratives and allow God to shape our own. This book is both a balm for the world-weary soul and a blueprint for living with purpose and peace."

Nicole Partridge, Journalist and Author.

A Picture and a thousand words

KELLIE HUTCHINSON

Ark House Press
arkhousepress.com

Front Cover photography by Deyaco Kamboozia

Scripture quotations marked GW are from **GOD's WORD® Translation (GW®) **, © 1995, 2003, 2013, 2014, 2019, 2020 by God's Word to the Nations Mission Society. All rights reserved.

Scripture quotations marked MSG are from **The Message**, a paraphrase of the Bible by Eugene H. Peterson, © 1993, 2002, 2018. Used by permission of NavPress, represented by Tyndale House

Scripture quotations marked NIV are from the **New International Version (NIV®) **. © [Insert relevant years, e.g., 1973, 1978, 1984, 2011] by Biblica, Inc.®. Used by permission. All rights reserved worldwide.

Scripture quotations marked GNT (or GNB) are from the **Good News Translation (GNT)**, formerly Today's English Version (TEV), © 1992 by American Bible Society. Used by permission.

Scripture quotations marked ERV are from the **Easy-to-Read Version (ERV)**, © 2006 by Bible League International. Used by permission.

Scripture quotations marked NLT are from the **New Living Translation (NLT)**. © 1996,2004,2015 by Tyndale House Foundation. Used by permission of Tyndale House Publishers, Inc.

Scripture quotations marked CEV are from the **Contemporary English Version (CEV)**, © 1991, 1992, 1995 by American Bible Society. Used by permission.

Scripture quotations marked WEB are from the **World English Bible (WEB)**, which is in the public domain. No permission required.

Cataloguing in Publication Data:
Title: A Picture And A Thousand Words
ISBN: 978-1-7643577-5-3 (pbk)
Subjects: REL012170 RELIGION / Christian Living / Personal Memoirs; REL012130 RELIGION / Christian Living / Women's Interests; REL012120 RELIGION / Christian Living / Spiritual Growth.

Design by initiateagency.com

A Thinker and Her Thoughts

These words are my own.
They will grow as I grow. Evolve as I evolve.
They are intended to uplift, not inflict.
May they do just that, like every good word should.

Like a gift to the world,
Is the right word at the right time
I hope this will be that word

The right word at the right time is like a custom-made piece of jewelry. Proverbs 25:11 (MSG)

Contents

God has had it with the proud. But takes delight in just plain people. So be content with who you are, and don't put on airs.

1 Peter 5:5 (MSG)

Ordinary *People*

─── ✦ ───

I am an ordinary person-from Earth's point of view, anyway.

It's nice to be an ordinary person.

Today, I ventured out into the world with one hand's nails painted pink with polish, while the other hand's nails remained bare.

I'd started painting them with my DIY shellac kit when life called.

So out I went, hands half-finished. My left hand a blank canvas, my right hand showing off its pretty pink sheen.

It was a work in progress.
But, honestly, aren't we all?

No one cared. No one noticed. No one commented.

I thoroughly enjoyed my day without any backlash from society. Ordinary people can do that, and I love that!

Would having two perfectly manicured hands have made me or my occasion more special anyway?

I didn't think about my nails once that day. I was too busy engaging in the world around me to worry about such a small percentage of my body.

Life can be enjoyable with or without perfect nails when you are ordinary. That is why I love ordinary things.

My hair is way overdue for a colour, and I have regrowth the size of Mount Everest. It's been more than eight weeks since I coloured my hair, and the greys are throwing a party. They are ecstatic to have been given the opportunity to see the light of day.

I'm usually the killjoy who crashes their parties at the onset. But right now, I am in a busy season of work and end-of-year preparations, so my hair must wait until I'm ready for it. A two-hour salon trip cannot be squeezed into my weekly agenda right now, even if I wish it could.

Since my hair doesn't run my show, I have put it in its place. On the waitlist. With the rest of my upkeep. When you are ordinary, things like hair can wait — especially when more exciting things in life are happening to pursue.

I venture out into the world with my regrowth.

I still feel beautiful and secure. People still say hello to me and embrace me warmly with their hugs and personal greetings. Not one person chastises me for coming out with less-than-perfect hair.

My hair probably makes their hair feel better if they are as time restricted as I am. There is relief all around. They secretly thank me for putting them at ease like this, though no words are exchanged. Perfect hair can be intimidating. My hair is giving them relief.

The world doesn't fall off its axis. The stars are not in disarray just because my hair is. My hair and I are just fine. We are blessing the world in an unorthodox way.

Life goes on wonderfully, hair regrowth and all.

I attended a family fun day that was raising money for a charity that day.
I shopped my own wardrobe and found something to wear from my already full, overflowing closet. I've worn the outfit multiple times. I love it.
It's comfortable, practical and looks good.

It's not high-end designer fashion. It's ordinary. But I'm not afraid of being ordinary, so I can wear it.

No one knew or cared that I'd worn the outfit before.
No one knew or cared if it was a brand.
In fact, nobody asked.

Why would they?
Ordinary people don't get asked such questions.

Is it suitable for the weather?
Maybe. But the questions about your attire stop there.

I love that I can live life like this. Simple and carefree when it comes to my attire.
Yes, I could go out tomorrow and look extra fabulous if I wanted and the occasion called for it. But ordinary can do, every other day.
Ordinary people can do that.

There is no pressure to look extraordinary.
Ordinary people don't get imposter syndrome.
They simply can be who they are.

Considering my nails, hair regrowth, and outfit right now, it's probably a good thing.

In hindsight, I don't think a designer dress would have made the occasion more memorable for me. In fact, I would have been bothered by all the dust and dirt wrecking my fashion investment, as the event was held outdoors at an airport.
I had none of those concerns.

I was there to support a good cause and interact with my community. I did just that.
I enjoyed that day, dressed casually and all.

If I had worn designer clothes, no one would have noticed anyway.
They were too busy supporting the cause of terminally ill children.
I think they would have smiled, knowing I invested money into the charity instead of a dress to wear for it.

I got a brand-new car once.
It was immaculate. Shiny, new, spotless.

It was extraordinary.

People commented on how lovely and beautiful it was.
I thought so too.

My perfect car had to stay perfect though, so apart from driving, it couldn't do much else.

I couldn't eat in it, nor could anyone else. You can't eat and leave crumbs and scraps in extraordinary things!

Drinks were off the table in my new car too.
Especially for my then two-year-old.

I think my two-year-old preferred our ordinary car, where she could drink her drinks, snack on her snacks, and bring home a truckload of sand from the beach.

Trips to the beach became torturous for me, trying to stop the sand and wet, salty bodies from destroying my extraordinary car. Sometimes I avoided the ordeal altogether. Wouldn't you if you had an extraordinary car that could get wrecked? The day it grew old and withered was celebrated. We could now do all the things we couldn't do when it was extraordinary. Like drink our drinks, eat our food, and bring back buckets of sand and shells from the beach.

To think of all those times, we remained thirsty and beach-deprived because of an extraordinary car.

That's why I love ordinary things now. Some things become too precious to be practical, and extraordinary things are often on that list.

A friend got married once. The bride's mother had a special cabinet full of special glasses, saved for special occasions. Those special ornaments had remained untouched and on display for decades, waiting for that 'special occasion' to arrive. The wedding day came and went, and the extraordinary glasses weren't used. I heard the bride questioning her mother: why weren't the special glasses used? What was more special than a daughter's wedding?

Sometimes we keep things for a special occasion, and that special occasion passes by and we miss the moment to use those extraordinary treasures anyway.

I don't have a special occasion cabinet. I use my special glasses daily because there is no time like the present and every day is special.

My friends are the *truest* kind of friends; they have been with me throughout the years. We've experienced all sorts of hurdles and joys together. We've celebrated each other's weddings and comforted each other through divorce. We've welcomed children into the world and mourned those that didn't make it all the way here. We've watched our children grow through good days and bad days. We shared our joys and triumphs. We shared our sorrows and tragedies. They have cheered for me in my winning seasons, and they encouraged me in my losing seasons. I have done the same for them. They are forever implanted in my heart as my tribe. We didn't need great hair, perfect figures, white teeth, and a designer wardrobe to create these invaluable moments and unbreakable bonds.

We did it dressed up and dressed down. We did it on good hair days, bad hair days, and no-hair days. We didn't have better days dressed up than dressed down. We brought our true selves to each moment, and that's all that mattered.

That's the thing about being ordinary-you have no doubt who your friends are and why they are there. After all, what else are you bringing to their table apart from your authentic, ordinary self? You are enough without any other trimmings. That's why I love ordinary people. There's no need for airs and graces. The love is authentic, genuine, real, and without a doubt.

But what of the billionaires? Are they surrounded by authentic, real, and genuine people?

Would a young, beautiful supermodel marry a significantly older man for love alone? Or does the love of wealth play a part? If he was poor would there be nuptials?

Is that authentic, genuine, and real love? Or just superficial affection? I'm not sure. Only God knows people's true heart motives, even if they fool themselves.

My house is ordinary too. I've lived in an extraordinary house before - for ten years. It was described as a manor. It had three bathrooms, five bedrooms, a 22-metre garage, and a huge entertainer's balcony and yard. It sat on top of a hill with all the other elite houses looking down on the ordinary community.

I wasn't happy in that extraordinary house, even though it was perfect and pristine in every way. If a house could make you happy, it would have. Today I'm happier in my downgraded house. My soul is at peace, and my cleaning time at a minimum.

The world told me I would need a big house to be happy. So, I worked hard for years to obtain one. But the company you keep can make your homelife miserable or amazing, no matter how grand or otherwise a house is. I said goodbye to both the grand house and the company, and now I love my ordinary life.

The Bible says it's better to live in a run-down shack than with a nagging spouse. I can testify to that. Though my house is far from a run-down shack, and my spouse did way more than nag.

It's not the home that I love so much now - it's the life I'm free to live in it. The freedom within its walls, the safety and shelter it offers. Who knew walking away from something extraordinary would give me these blessings? Who knew leaving extraordinary to gain ordinary was the silver lining? It was though. For me.

Ordinary people smile when they look at you. They aren't worried about new wrinkles forming on their face, so they are happy to stretch their smile lines to embrace you.

I've heard of an extraordinary celebrity who refused to smile for the very same reason. I wish someone would tell her how beautiful a smile makes a face. It more than compensates for any wrinkles that may form from the habit of smiling.

I love to smile and know the benefits of doing so. Because I am ordinary, I can indulge in these benefits. I smile at every person I see. I'm not worried about the world commenting on my smile lines or my imperfect teeth.

Since when did a smile require perfect teeth? And are those without perfect teeth doomed to frown?

Ordinary people can do what they please, so I smile. Others are grateful for my smiles. I'm sure they are because they almost always smile in return.

I work with people with neurological developmental disabilities. I have worked in this field for many years. If having a disability makes you less than ordinary, these people didn't get the memo. They are the happiest people I know, and we have the most extraordinary days at work. I thrive off their all-inclusive happy energy. I love their unfiltered simplicity and the good vibes they radiate. I love the way they interpret life and certain situations. It makes me smile a lot. They smile a lot too.

I guess you're not worried about smile lines when you have bigger problems to worry about, like day-to-day living. They are not worried about fashion, appearances, hair regrowth, or manicured nails. They are not worried about career progression, financial accumulation, or anything else neurotypical people tend to worry about. They simply live. Smelling the roses, chasing the butterflies, and asking the most profound questions. I guess that's why they are some of my favourite people. If the world would let them, they could teach the world a lot.

The year is turning into 2025, and my heart is thriving and full of hope and joy for this year ahead. I'm not sure how the extraordinary people's hearts are doing, but every day I hear of a new celebrity suiciding, overdosing on drugs, or admitting themselves into rehabilitation, so I'm guessing some of them are not faring that well in the land of extraordinary.

I'm starting to doubt that extraordinary will make our lives amazing. Especially when 'ordinary' works so wonderfully for me. I feel I could be a blessing to the world with my findings and message. If the world would heed me.

Extraordinary people might think they are lacking nothing, while ordinary people can see every mark and milestone of living that they are actually missing out on. I wouldn't trade places with a housewife of Beverly Hills for all the money in this world. You can't buy class. You can't purchase grace or swipe a credit card for morals or kindness. But these are the things that truly make your life rich.

I like dressing up for special occasions. I shop for a dress, put on hair and eyelash extensions, and spend a little extra time on my makeup and presentation. I transform from an average caterpillar to a beautiful butterfly. People comment that I look extraordinary. I feel it too, though I don't let it go to my head, knowing ordinary awaits me tomorrow. People don't compliment me like that any other day when I'm showing up as my ordinary self. Do I need such compliments every day? No! So, I'm happy to stay ordinary every other day and save extraordinary for a special occasion. It would be exhausting to aim for extraordinary every day. There is no time for that in my day-to-day schedule, and the time invested would not be worth it for the odd compliment. I decide the world around me can focus on my other qualities every other day. Like my kindness, friendliness, wisdom, and happy disposition.

I'm glad I have other qualities I can call on, apart from my physical appearance. Imagine if my worth came purely from my looks. One day I will be old and grey, and then what will I think of myself?

My spirit will always be extraordinary, and age and life won't wither it. I'm glad I invest in my spirit. I think I get the best returns from doing so. Much more than the odd, extraordinary comment someone would offer my physical appearance in my made-up moments.

I pray, I read, I invest in my emotional intelligence and personal development. This has served me well and is the reason I smile.

As I get older, they may not call me physically beautiful anymore. And that will be the call for me to graciously call someone else those words and pass the baton to the youth. But they will still call me calm, happy, wise, thoughtful, generous, and lovely. Aren't these beautiful words? These qualities will still define me, though 'physically beautiful' may be scrubbed off the list.

I'm not scared of that day.
Because I will still be extraordinary even when the world won't recognize it.

Sometimes, if I'm ever intimidated by someone's beauty and youth and feel the weight of their haughty stares, I just picture them when they are older. I imagine them in forty year's time, take a sigh of relief, and realize we will all be there one day. Old and ordinary (if we are fortunate enough to live that long). Knowing that, I'm even happier to give people their moment of glory, especially when I know it is fleeting. I tell them they are beautiful, to enjoy the moment and intimidation flees.

I love that my wardrobe isn't stretched to capacity, nor is my credit card, because I'm content with the ordinary. Committing to extraordinary full-time would get expensive. I feel I look just as good wearing my low-end everyday fashions as I would in high end designer. I'm happier too, knowing there wasn't a hefty price tag attached to each day's look.

My cousin once told me that clothes weren't a good investment. I believed him, so I put my spare change into the property market and my savings.

It was the best advice ever. My house is paid off, I have no debts, and I am financially free. I did all this while wearing ordinary clothes and shoes. I'm not sure if I would have been able to achieve financial freedom if I needed designer clothes for every occasion. I'm also certain designer clothes would not have given me a million-dollar return like my property investment did.

No one would know I am financially well off, looking at my day-to-day attire. When you are content with ordinary, you don't need to flaunt extraordinary.

I'm not sure if those wearing designer shoes, clothes, and jewellery have paid off their credit cards or mortgages and are financially free like me. I guess that is the million-dollar question.

Being financially free is an exhilarating feeling. A shopping spree has never given me that kind of inner peace and joy.

There is beauty in being ordinary.
There is freedom when the world isn't commenting on your every move. That is why I'm content with ordinary things.

We were all born ordinary, but the world decided to promote some people as extraordinary along the way. People seemed to love the idea of that, so strive for the title, not knowing the huge weights and impossible standards attached. They now must be perfect because they are extraordinary.

Carrying huge weights around on your shoulders has never made any soul happy. I feel compelled to tell people this so they could strive to carry the lesser load that comes with being ordinary and brings more joy.

"Perfection is the enemy of progress," said Winston Churchill once. I am all for progress, so I am happily imperfect and flawed and have no desire to enter the realm of the extraordinaire.

I think I'm one of the happiest people in this world. I did a resilience test recently and scored in the top 1 percent of happy people. I answered each question truthfully and honestly. Why would I fool myself? I believed the results of the test because I feel content, happy, and in love with my life in every way. I love where I live. I love what I do. I love my family, friends, partner and child. I love God and others.

Like everyone, I have had good, bad, sad and ugly days. Anyone who lives on earth will encounter the same. The earthly experience doesn't say, "Oh, you are rich, or smart, or popular, or pretty, or famous. I will leave you alone and not trouble you."

Life's challenges will target everybody, no matter what your demographic, social status, or financial disposition.

We will all face struggles, temptations, pain, heartbreak, grief, and loss.

Jesus said, *"In this godless world you will continue to experience difficulties. But take heart! I've conquered the world."* John 16:33 (MSG)

I think it was a call to be brave and overcome too!

Yes, I am ordinary.
But I have scored high in the test of resilience and life.
Maybe I am extraordinary after all - just not by earth's definition of the word.

"God chose what the world considers ordinary and what it despises—what it considers to be nothing—in order to destroy what it considers to be something."
1 Corinthians 1:28 (GWT)

It's nice to know, while the world says you must be outstanding, amazing, and extraordinary-God delights in ordinary people.

The *Happiest*

Have you ever noticed the lack of inhibitions young children possess?

It was swimming season. Every day for two weeks, my daughter's kindergarten class was bussed to a local pool to learn to swim or brush up on their water skills.

In Australia, swimming lessons are prioritised, since we're surrounded by beaches, lakes, and water.

No one in the class was worrying about body image or how they looked in their swimsuits. The children weren't comparing body types, swimsuits, or fleshy imperfections. There was no frantic dieting or gym prep in the lead-up. My six-year-old daughter was downing chocolate cake and Nutella all the way through swim season without a care in the world - completely unfazed that she would be wearing swim wear.

There they all were, bellies out, goggles on, enjoying the gift of swimming and water. Uninhibited. Present. Simply being what they were made to be, without comparison, competition, or shame. It was refreshing and liberating.

Fast forward a few years, and things will begin to change. The pressure to fit in and look a certain way will start to overshadow the fun. Some kids will become so self-conscious they'll sit out of swimming class altogether, choosing the sidelines over the pool.

There will be many reasons why they'll tell themselves they can't participate anymore.
Maybe they'll believe their swimwear isn't fashionable enough.
Maybe they'll be self-critical of their body shape.
Maybe they'll dread what the chlorine will do to their hair or how the water might mess up their made-up face.
Maybe puberty will hit, and the ingrown hairs or hairy legs will be too much to handle.

But really - were we designed to look like Victoria Secret models just to enjoy the gift of swimming? Or was the gift of water freely given to all of us to be refreshed by?

Afterall, the skinny eel shares the same ocean with the massive whale. No one's telling the big whale it has no right to swim in the ocean until it shrinks in size. No one's scorning the eel for not taking up enough space and looking too thin. No one's laughing at the hairy otter.
Animals appear to live freely and carelessly without concern for their body image. They simply *are* what they are, by design and default, and no thought goes into changing or judging that.

Is the hippopotamus worrying about its large circumference?
Is the elephant stressing about its wrinkled skin?

They just go on being brilliant, celebrating their other qualities. The elephant's magnificent memory. The hippo's incredible skin.

Should we learn from the animal kingdom where all creatures accept themselves big or small? Should we learn from children who splish and splash with glee enjoying the simple things in life without complications, and comparisons?

There's a children's book I used to read to my daughter called *I Am the Happiest* by Anna Shuttlewood. In it, animals boast about what makes them special. The giraffe boasts about being the tallest, the hedgehog about being the spikiest, the frog about being the greenest.

But then there's a little raccoon who doesn't join the competition.
He simply smiles and says, "I'm glad giraffe is the tallest, and frog is the greenest, and hedgehog the spikiest. I'm glad. I am the happiest."

It inspires me to look around and freely give everyone their crowns: Yes, you can be the prettiest.
Yes, you can have the most online followers.
Yes, you can have the most flawless skin.
Yes, you can be the fittest, the richest, the best-dressed.

I'm happy for you all. Truly.
For I'm aiming to be the happiest.

Being the happiest doesn't come from external things. It comes from inner peace, self-acceptance, and gratitude. That's what carries you through life - not what the world has sold us.

"Each one should test their own actions. Then they can take pride in themselves alone, without comparing themselves to someone else, for each should carry their own load."
Galatians 6:4 (NIV)

You'll never find joy trying to carry someone else's load while neglecting your own.

We all come in different shapes and sizes, and everybody is beautiful. So, love your body. It's the vessel you have been given to get you through this life. It lives, breathes, moves, touches, smells, sees, feels, and hears. There is beauty and wonder in everybody. We are all works of art and a priceless creation. Remember that the next time you are questioning your beauty. You don't need a perfect body to get through this life. You need a healthy one.

"You can admire someone else's beauty without questioning your own." Unknown

You're blessed when you're content with just who you are—no more, no less. That's the moment you find yourselves proud owners of everything that can't be bought.
Matthew 5:5 (MSG)

$\mathcal{Life}$ Lines

"You get wrinkles because you've been given the honour of growing old," a mother once said to me regarding aging skin.

This woman had been battling multiple sclerosis for 15 years, and the fact that she was still standing was a miracle. Growing old was truly a privilege for someone with her condition, wrinkles, and all.

I loved that quote, and before long, I found myself repeating it often, especially when friends would complain about their aging looks.

What started as a simple quote gradually evolved. Each time I shared it, more words seemed to pour out naturally, such as:

"You have wrinkles because you got to spend years sunbaking guilt-free-before society knew any better.
You have wrinkles because you raised children and survived their teenage years.
You have wrinkles in preparation for the joy of grandchildren.
You have wrinkles because you've been selected to experience the beauty and wisdom of old age.

You have wrinkles because you're brave enough to wear them, instead of hiding behind injections and paralyzers.

You have wrinkles because you've lived, laughed, cried, smiled, and expressed yourself. Embrace these stories of your life, etched in your skin. For they are your *lifelines*."

Why do we despise our aging skin when we can wear our lifelines with pride? We've earned everyone one of those lines, like trophies. They are proof of our existence on planet earth. Proof that we have laughed and smiled and felt emotions. Proof that we have walked this earth for a while gaining experience, knowledge, and wisdom. Our eyes have seen a lot, our skin has weathered even more. Every line marks our survival as we've triumphed through every year and gained another one.

Should we feel pressured to keep our youth forever, as if aging were a flaw to fix?

Couldn't we embrace every season of our life including old age?

Why has aging become the chapter the world wants to skip, when it could be the best read?

Why are we being taught to fear the very season that was once honoured and revered?

To a world that tells us we shouldn't embrace our age, we can say *'We do'*.
To a world that wants to profit from our imperfections and insecurities, we can say '*We won't*'
To a world that tells us youth is beauty and aging is decline,
We can simply block our ears and age anyway.

Our wrinkles don't need to change, our thinking does.
Summer doesn't cling to spring, and winter doesn't stay fixated on autumn.
Each season passes in its time and the new season brings its own kind of
beauty and blessing. There is joy to be found in every season of life if we're
optimistic enough to receive it.

Let the youth have their moment in the sun; each of us has stood there
once, before stepping into the next season of life. In time, they too will
grow older- if they're afforded the gift of extended time. So, no one should
get too comfortable in the season of youth, too proud of appearances, too
quick to dismiss the elderly. Because age eventually finds us all. And if we've
built our worth on something that fades, what a troubling day that will be
for our flesh.

Aging is a privilege not everyone is afforded.
So those who are- celebrate!

This world needs every kind of person, and the elderly have their revered,
honoured place.

Yes, one day, we may look in the mirror
and no longer recognize the aged face looking back at us.
Our skin may sag, stretch, wither, and fade.
We may become slower, more forgetful. Our bones may ache.

Since the fall, we were never designed to be eternal on this earth.
None of us were.
This earth - with its heartbreaks and sorrows- is not good enough for our
spirits to endure forever.
Therefore, we age.

And although I sometimes wish we could stay on earth forever,
I've never seen heaven, or the afterlife.
No one comes back- so it must be exceptional.
I trust that God has made eternity so.

> *Charm is deceptive, and beauty is fleeting; but a woman who*
> *fears the Lord is to be praised.*
> *Honor her for all that her hands have done, and let her works*
> *bring her praise at the city gate.* Proverbs 31:30 (NIV)

When beauty fades, that's when the work of your hands can speak louder.
Your flesh may no longer draw attention
but your kindness and service still can.

My grandmother was praised for the work of her hands:
The endless Sunday roasts she made for the entire extended family.
The Saturday lunches, the Christmas dinners.
The way she held us all together. Building and blessing her family
community, with lolly jars and homemade biscuits. With table tennis
games she could still win at 90 and blankets she crocheted with her very
own hands. A legacy built from faith, and love.

My mother is praised for the work of her hands:
Raising five children.
Loving many grand ones.
heavily involved in our lives—even at 71.

The praise didn't come from wrinkle-free skin,
but from lives poured out in love.

May the work of my hands reward me, long after my beauty fades.
May my actions generate praise, long after my reflection can.

Blessed *are* those who live long enough to grow old.
To see their children's children.
There are graveyards full of those who didn't get to see.
And a world full of people who wish they did.

Wrinkles and all.

It would be lovely to witness a world less obsessed with appearances and more obsessed with the inner qualities of the soul. Maybe future generations will get back to the basics and build this braver world.
I'll be long gone by then.
But I'll be cheering from afar.

"More power to those brave enough to embrace their lifelines."

Beyond *Beauty*

Life is fleeting.
Like a flower, we bloom, flourish, and slowly fade.
No matter how radiant we are today, time will eventually dim our beauty.
Flawlessness isn't forever. No matter how well-groomed we are, or amazing our skin care routine is.

Models and influencers will grow old, and their names, once trending, will be replaced by newer, fresher faces.
Actors and superstars will have their moments, then the curtains will close on their parades.
Trendsetters of today will be surpassed by the new trendsetters of tomorrow.
Influence is temporary. Fame is brief.
Ten generations from now, no one will remember their names.
So much of it was… in vain. Like a chasing of the wind.
We live, then we die.

It's the only guarantee we have in this life.

That there will be an end to this earthly experience through death.

Shouldn't that stir us to live more?

More purposefully, more mindfully? More thoughtfully?

You would think so. Though we tend to live in complete denial of that day.

It's pushed aside, like it will never happen to us. So, we continue to live for today. Planting our seeds, growing our crops, reaping our harvest, oblivious to an end date. We think we have forever, till that day catches most people unaware. Like it did my dad. One minute here, the next minute gone. Midway through his lifeline. The lifetime cut short.

There were still young children to raise. A family that loved and needed him. He didn't get a say when his time was up. Neither did we. We think we have forever on earth, but we're only guaranteed today.

I blamed God for my father's death when I was young and naïve. 'God took him too young' I thought. Now I know God doesn't kill anyone. The earth does, our choices do, the stress of living here does, the toxins we're exposed to, the people, the polluted planet.

Death takes us from this earth, then God steps in and offers us eternal life in a better world that can't destroy us. God wipes the tears, heals the suffering, rights all the wrongs and makes all things new. If you look at it like that, death doesn't look so bad. It is just a pathway to somewhere greater.

On that day, when the next life comes knocking, will it matter if I weighed 55 kilos or had paid off my car?
Will it count for anything if I had a prestigious career, or a swollen bank account? Could my savings save me then?
Would any debt be able to drown me?

No.

Because when I leave this earth,
None of it will matter. The earthly experience and all it entails will be over when eternity steps in.

In the scales of eternity, possessions and appearances will hold no weight. Only who we are and who we belong to will matter.

The world is hurting. It's messy, broken and struggling under the weight of real problems. The news headlines we skim over every day is someone's sad reality. The world serves us suffering at times. People are searching for hope in a world that often feels like it's falling apart.

Does this hurting world care about our designer fashion, material accumulations and skincare routines? Does this hurting world need our every waking moment recorded and captured with a perfect filter for them to view? What are we trying to prove or accomplish with our reels? Are we meant to be wasting so much time and energy investing in an online world when the real world is longing for our presence? Desperate for us to show up resembling courage, compassion, love and positive change?

As a woman, I sometimes wonder if our foremothers are quietly rolling their eyes at us.
Did we sell out?

They fought for the right to vote.
For equality.
For a voice. A chance to be heard. A say in making the world better.

And here we are, their legacy… fighting for flawless figures and fame.
They were concerned for the future of womankind. And we-their future-
seem to be mostly consumed with… ourselves.

Who's the hottest? Who's trending? Who has the best hair, face, and body?

Surely, we can raise the bar.
Surely, there are worthier benchmarks to reach for.

Sometimes, I get these *crazy* ideas, that maybe more is required of us than
good looks and designer bodies.
That our brilliant minds were made for more than curating content and
chasing validation.
(And yes, I know many women *are* doing extraordinary things.)

But there's still been some crazy crazes in the name of beauty, and we
continue to create them and chase them.

Remember the corset era?
Apparently, women of the French court saw corsets as "indispensable to the
beauty of the female figure."
Indispensable? Really?
Food is indispensable. Water is indispensable. But corsets?

The corset craze lasted centuries.
Women everywhere squeezed themselves in.
Heaven forbid they let their lungs breathe!
Isn't it concerning how someone, somewhere, decided an hourglass figure
was "beautiful"- and the world followed?
That's centuries of altered stomachs and suffocated ribs.

Did anyone ever stop to say, "We've lost the plot"?
Was anyone brave enough to resist?

According to Wikipedia eventually something did stop the sale of corsets-
World War I.
In 1917, the U.S. War Industries Board asked women to stop buying
corsets to free up metal for war production.
Turns out, an hourglass figure isn't much use in a world at war.
That move freed up 28,000 tonnes of metal- enough to build two
battleships.
Can you imagine what those women could have accomplished over the
centuries before if they'd focused on a worthier cause than waistlines.

And yet… here we are.
Corsets have returned- just with sleeker branding.
Tummy trainers. Shapewear. Spanx.
(Again- no judgement. I get it.)

So far, I've resisted.
But if everyone around me starts walking around looking like living,
breathing hourglasses, the pressure to conform will rise.
If abnormal becomes the new normal… should I follow?

Should I, like the women before me, empower the craze to carry on?
Should I spend my energy on tummy trainers and trends?

One thing I've learned along the way is that changing how we look on the
outside doesn't always bring peace on the inside. It's not a lost cause to work
on appearances. We all want to look good and feel good. But polishing a

car doesn't help a car go anywhere if the tanks empty. A beautiful exterior cannot compensate an empty soul.

We often admire people's cars, clothes, homes, waistlines- but in the end it's not about how things look. It's about where they are taking you and how they are serving you. With that said, even a humble car and modest body has the potential to take someone somewhere meaningful.

The best outcomes always come from working on the mind and spirit. Wisdom and truth will teach you that.

Each year, I just want to put my best foot forward.
And no, it's not the one with the designer shoe chasing another trend (though a designer shoe may be here and there).
It's the one walking on purpose.
Towards something that matters.
One intentional step at a time.

And if someone doesn't like my outfit as I walk?
If I end up on the worst-dressed list in people's minds for not giving my attire the highest priority? Should I even care? I'll remind myself: I wasn't born to look good.
I was born to *do* good. My stride will get stronger. My purpose clearer.

Maybe I'll wear a vintage thrift to my next big event.
And donate what I would've spent on fashion to charity.
Because you know what?
I can still be sensational with or without the price tag and there's some wonderful causes to support.

"Does the dress make the woman, or the woman make the dress?" someone once said.

I believe the woman makes the dress if she wears it with carefree confidence and kindness.

And that kind of confidence?

It doesn't come from clothes.

It comes from soul work.

You can look ordinary and still live an *extraordinary* life.

Because beauty isn't the only quality worth cultivating.

It's not all about outer beauty. We have many other qualities and attributes to work with as well. Let's not forget these. They're the real tools that will get us where we're meant to be going.

Start with your health.

Mental. Physical. Spiritual.

And build from there.

That's what makes you extraordinary.

> *"What matters is not your outward appearance—the styling of your hair, the jewellery you wear, the cut of your clothes—but your inner disposition. Cultivate inner beauty, the gentle, gracious kind that God delights in."* 1 Peter 3:3 (MSG)

God delights in our inner beauty.

The world desperately needs to see more of it. There's an abundance of outer beauty in the world. But can the beautiful hearts please rise up?

Can the Real Me Please Stand Up?

We hide behind our makeup,
And manufactured smiles,
We cover up what's real.
With foundation, gloss, and style.

We hide behind our fashions,
And filtered online reels,
Flaunt perfect lives through fragile screens,
But none of it is real.

We hide behind our diets,
Deny our natural size,
Convince ourselves that we prefer
salad to steak and fries.

We bite our tongues and censor words,
The truth we dare not say,
Afraid of being scorned and mocked,
our courage fades away.

Is this how life was meant to be
Exchanging joy for trends?
Consumed by shallow standards,
while laughter slowly ends.

We're busy chasing what's "in trend,"
Too scared to just be free,
So focused on becoming her,
We lose who we should be.

Despite our perfect selfies
We're still not having fun
Fixated on our image
While our souls the broken one.

What we wear, or how we fit
Why's it such an issue?
Shouldn't we be more concerned
About our soul's condition?

The truth is, we keep hiding
Behind a polished front,
There's more to life than looking good.
Can the real me please stand up?

—Kellie Hutchinson

There's More To Me Than What You *See*

We should all give ourselves permission to shine- especially in a world that so often tries to dim our light and feels more at ease in the shadows. We should also give ourselves permission *not* to shine so brightly. To be dull, to rest, to be real. To not always look like porcelain Barbie dolls stepping straight out of a magazine with perfectly sculpted and polished everything.

Today, the pressure to appear picture-perfect is relentless. Perfect bodies, flawless skin, impeccable makeup, manicured nails, pearly white teeth, designer outfit. It's a hard expectation to live up to. The pressures on the younger generation are intense.

But when did the flesh become more important than the soul?
When did appearances gain so much power and inner qualities so little? It wasn't always that way.

One day, I decided to leave the house with messy hair and barely any makeup. If I were a celebrity, the tabloids would have had a field day. We've all seen the headlines: "Stars Without Makeup!" followed by harsh photos and harsher commentary.

But when did it become acceptable to publicly shame people for being human or natural?

And so, we let the bullies win.
We let faceless people dictate how we live and impact our day-to-day lives.
We remain tied to chains of perfection, never daring to step out undone again.
We stay bound and contained to perfect appearances and the burden of maintaining them.

We allow others to dictate how we dress, how often we do our hair, and what "acceptable" looks like. We fear the comments. We fear the lack of likes.
But why are we giving such power to people who don't deserve it?
Why are we letting small-minded, mean-spirited voices define how we live?

Couldn't we simply choose not to indulge in mean written words and find something more enlightening to read?

The media may be having a field day over your bad hair day and weight gain, but the rest of society is actually relieved when celebrities look human.
Maybe you are being just as inspirational on your bad days than your good.
Maybe you're being more?

Shouldn't we seek out the voices cheering us on for being brave enough to show our imperfections, instead of listening to the ones that want to condemn and conform us?
Perfection is an illusion anyway.

I give myself permission to be real.

To be ordinary, average, human.

To have breakouts that sometimes won't go away, skin that acts up at times and hair that misbehaves.
I give myself permission not to be toned or tanned or perfectly tailored.
I give my hair permission to be dry or oily or just not that great.
I give myself permission to be *who I am in each moment*—no performance required. I can arrive to any occasion however I feel fit. No one gets to dictate how many hours I must spend preparing, or the price I should pay to arrive. My arrival is enough, in body and spirit. I am greater than my image. There is more to me than what you see. I will bring meaningful conversations. You will feel my good energy and experience my love. Kindness will ooze out of my soul and you will catch my joy and laughter. That is more precious than a flawless image.

We weren't created to walk through life looking like mannequins in a window front display. With no character, individuality, or charisma. We weren't born to be slaves to all these things we must do in preparation just to arrive somewhere. Nails, hair, skin, lashes, tan.
Our bodies are tools, not trophies. A tool for the spirit it carries.
Is the tool greater than the soul using it?

> *Is a saw more important than the one who saws with it?*
> *A club doesn't lift up a person; a person lifts a club.*
> Isaiah 10:15 (GNT)

There was a young girl at my workplace who once skipped our end of year work Christmas celebrations. When I asked her why she didn't make it, she said she had tried on 20 different outfits, and none of them felt right so she stayed at home.

I remember thinking- I wouldn't have cared what attire she came in, I would have just loved her company. My heart felt sad for a beautiful young girl requiring the perfect outfit just to arrive somewhere. Didn't she know she could arrive anyway? Imperfectly dressed and all.

What had made her believe she had to look a certain way just to show up? Did we love her for her dress sense? No! Her image? Hardly. Didn't she know her presence was the real gift- not her packaging?

This is what the pursuit of perfection does. It steals our joy, our time, our moments.
It convinces us we aren't enough. It robs us and others of connection.

That old saying, *"Sticks and stones may break my bones, but words will never hurt me"* is a lie. There are countless humans still reeling from ill spoken words. *Words kill, words give life; they're either poison or fruit.* Proverbs 18:21 (MSG)

They affect our lives. Unkind words try to take root in our lives and if they do they grow into weeds that choke out our ability to flourish.

But haters will continue to hate, no matter how dressed up we are or how brightly we shine.
So appeasing haters is not the answer; rejecting their hate-filled words is.

That is what is within our control.
You get to decide what enters your heart.
You get to choose whose voice matters or what words to heed and believe. WWJTY (What would Jesus tell you) Something wonderful, life giving and awe inspiring no doubt. Something that will grow and bear good fruit.

There's only a handful of people that speak into my life. Those who've earned that right with love, consistency, and wisdom. Even then, I still weigh each word and come to my own conclusions. Why would I give that sacred space to strangers who may have bitter hearts, false opinions or hidden agendas? Who knows if they are educated or not educated enough in manners and human decency to make comments good enough to heed? Who knows if they have a spirit from God?

The world judges a book by its cover and misses out on some brilliant reads. Some seize books with pretty covers that will prove disappointing to read in the long run.

Not all books are presented with the fanciest of covers. But turn some pages, and you may find the gold.

God sees the whole story — every word, every chapter.

God also doesn't judge by appearances but by the heart.

The Bible says the devil is a liar and a hater. The hater of our souls.
So why live in agreement with haters or liars? They don't get to judge our worth or hand out our labels. Reserve that honour for God. God is the judge of our worth.

> *Take up the shield of faith, with which you can extinguish*
> *all the flaming arrows of the evil one.* Ephesians 6:16 (NIV)

We don't have to live fearing every word someone might say if we show up raw, real, or undone.
Fear is exhausting.

Perfection is expensive.
It costs time, energy, joy, and peace. It is stressful to maintain, and at the end of the day, it doesn't offer much in dividends.

You don't enjoy life more when you're flawless. You don't bear more fruit.
You just become a brighter target for jealousy, envy and hate.

You will never be "good enough" for some people, so it's a fruitless pursuit living for the likes of people.

But *you* can be the one who speaks life.
You *can* be the one who gives compliments freely.
It doesn't make you less - it makes you *more*.
It takes a secure heart to lift someone else up and offer them kindness.
It really *is* better to give than to receive. (Acts 20:35)

The Bible says we overcome evil with good.
So speak good. Let people feel lighter after encountering you.

Even those who seem flawless are battling something.
Even the most perfect-looking people need life-giving words.
Fiery darts hit beautiful people too.
No one is immune to hate.
No one is above the need for love. So, strive to be the love.

One day, I won't be remembered for my hair or skin or how toned my body was.
The world will forget my appearance.
But those I've loved and encouraged, they'll remember *me*.
Not for how I looked, but for who I was and how they felt in my presence.

The people changing the world for the better aren't obsessing over their looks.

They're too busy building, healing, creating and serving.

They don't have time to fear the opinions of spectators sitting down, doing nothing, in their judgement seats.

True judgment comes from God who knows all the inner and outer workings of our lives and can't be tempted to show partiality based on wealth, status, charm, and pretty exteriors.

That's a relief for ordinary people.

The extraordinary and the ordinary have this in common: the Lord made them both and will judge them both.

There really is more to us than what you see.

There is the inner working of the heart to consider when weighing up one's beauty.

I'm glad God judges us with the overall picture in mind.

God once said to a prophet who was choosing the obvious choice to be king and overlooking the not-so-obvious:

> *"Do not consider his appearance or his height, for I have rejected him. The LORD does not look at the things people look at. People look at the outward appearance, but the LORD looks at the heart."*
> 1 Samuel 16:7 (NIV)

If that is the case, best get to work on our hearts and become more beautiful where it will ultimately count.

The *Thief*

You put on your best outfit. You feel unstoppable. Your shoes are shining, your makeup is flawless. You feel sensational. You are confident and ready to take on the world.

But on your way to world domination, you cross paths with someone more dazzling, more immaculately dressed and more put together than you.

What happens next?

A great robbery is what happens next!

A robbery of your confidence and self-worth.

Suddenly you don't feel so spectacular. Your outfit isn't as sharp, your makeup is falling short, along with everything else. Inadequacy starts creeping in. The spark has gone, your confidence diminished. Suddenly you don't feel so sensational. You feel unworthy, you want to go home. Your night is now lacking and so are you. You start thinking about all the things you need to improve on now… more fashionable clothes, shinier shoes, more time at the gym, better skin, and hair care.
You were ready to take on the world, till you realised you weren't.

What was the culprit? Comparison.

The thief called Comparison.

Comparison steals from us, quietly and without mercy.

It takes away the joy of our own uniqueness and replaces it with insecurity and a sense of lack.

But there is freedom in embracing who we truly are and finding contentment in our own journey and person if we can just get free from comparisons.

Beauty comes in every form.
Would the moon compare itself to the sun? Would the sea feel inferior to the mountain? Would the tree envy the flower? What a tragedy if they did. The world would lose its sunlight, its moonlight, and the shade of its trees, if they all tried to be something they weren't.

In the same way, when you deny your authentic self, the world is robbed of you.

Walk boldly in your own worth. Love who you are. No one else can fill your shoes quite like you can. You weren't meant to walk in anyone else's shoes, no matter how pretty they may be.

> *The clay doesn't ask, "Why did you make me this way? Where are the handles?* Isaiah 45:9 (CEV)

The clay just needs to enjoy being clay. Don't worry about the handles. If you needed handles for your journey, you would have been given them.

Embrace the beauty of your own unique design. Be who we were made to be without comparing yourself to others. You have everything you need to live *your* best life. Not one thing is lacking.

Comparison breeds both pride and shame- neither of which serve us.

> *Let's just go ahead and be what we were made to be, without enviously or pridefully comparing ourselves with each other, or trying to be something we aren't.* Romans 12:6 (MSG)

Real Women Have Stretch Marks

I don't mean to be stereotypical and put everybody in a box. Maybe you're in the rare, minute percentile that have managed to go through life without accumulating any stretch marks.

If you did or didn't - *in the case of those stretch marks* - good for you. I shall change the title to: *Real Women Don't Always Have Stretch Marks—But the Rest of Us Do.*

I personally have a rather nice and large collection of stretch marks that I've been secretly hiding behind my jeans and modest beach boardies for decades now.
I guess the secret's out.
I shall finally (and wholeheartedly) take responsibility for them.
Yes, they are mine.

The truth is, I feel so liberated - like I'm finally ready to proudly take my post as the poster girl for stretch marks.

In a world of editing, photoshopping, and filtered selfies that show us at our best and conceal our imperfections, I thought I'd do the world a favour and show myself *real.*
As I am.
As I come.

It's liberating to wear our imperfections with confidence and strength.
I have learned to love and embrace these stretch lines. I hardly even notice them anymore. To think I spent years hiding them, covering them, pretending they weren't there when I should have been displaying them like art.

For many years, they shamed me.
And not just my skin.
They scarred my self-esteem.
My confidence to wear swimwear, my body image. They made me second-guess my beauty.

It seems crazy to me now that I'm older and wiser. Why did I let a few stretch marks hold so much weight on my net worth, when they should have held so little?

Time and *age* are wonderful things, because with them, some powers have diminished. Diminished to the point where imperfections no longer bother me.
They are mine, and I've embraced them completely.
They no longer affect my mood, or my confidence, or my ability to get naked.

I don't need to live in fear of anyone finding them anymore.

To think I could've wasted years and money trying to fade them, fix them, improve them, erase them, when they weren't even going to be an issue for me one day.

The answer was acceptance and the realisation that I don't need a *perfect* body to get through this life. I need a *healthy* one. A *capable* one. A *strong* one.

The body is here to serve so much more than our pride and ego. The body is here to do so much more than shame us.

I am not going to waste another second of my life trying to perfect my body at the price of my well-being or wallet. The body is what it is. I simply love it, for the value it brings into my life, for the tasks it helps me do, for how it carries me through each day. It is strong, it is dependable, it is worthy to be appreciated.

So, I wear my stretch marks proudly.
I've moved the benchmark of perfection right back down the ladder-where it always should have been. An *impossible* target I no longer need to reach.

With time, beauty fades. And with that, our expectations shift too.
We will let go of the things that used to matter so much, because we realise, they matter so little now. We'll find love in all our imperfections.

Will your 90-year-old self worry about the stretch marks on her thighs, when there will be a million other lines mapping her face?

Good health will take priority then, as it always should have. This revelation will eventually find us all.

With time, the goal will change. The original goals won't matter.
The season to chase beauty will pass.
And in the rear-view mirror, we'll see all our vain pursuits for what they were-
Wasted energy.
Mental clutter.
Joy stolen from present moments.

We didn't need to change the imperfection.
We needed to change the *lens and focus*.
We didn't need to change the weakness. We needed to shift the *thought*.
We needed to affirm ourselves in all our weaknesses and imperfections and love ourselves, regardless.

To think, for all those years, I was so inhibited I wouldn't wear a bikini, despite having a beautiful, toned, healthy body.
All because I feared what someone might think of a few stretch marks.

But history books won't record the imperfections of my skin.
The ones who saw them would either judge them — or be empowered to show their imperfections too.

Why waste this journey on earth worrying about things that won't matter in the future? Including people's judgements

Looking back, I see wasted opportunity.
To have loved myself fully.
To have been real in each moment.

Real people have imperfections.
Why waste or hide them?

Physical beauty is *not* the most important tool for a good, prosperous, fruitful life.
Physical beauty is also *temporary.*

Enjoy your youth. Enjoy your beauty.

Realising - There's more in your soul than what's reflected in your mirror.
Realising - A kind, friendly, loving inner disposition is far greater than any flawless exterior.
If you have to choose, **choose inner beauty**.
It's the most beautiful thing of all.

> *"Don't fuss about what's on the table at mealtimes or if the clothes in your closet are in fashion. There is far more to your inner life than the food you put in your stomach, more to your outer appearance than the clothes you hang on your body.*
> *Look at the ravens, free and unfettered, not tied down to a job description, carefree in the care of God. And you count far more.*
> *Has anyone by fussing before the mirror ever gotten taller by so much as an inch? If fussing can't even do that, why fuss at all? Walk into the fields and look at the wildflowers. They don't fuss with their appearance—but have you ever seen color and design quite like it? The ten best-dressed men and women in the country look shabby alongside them.*

If God gives such attention to the wildflowers, most of them never even seen, don't you think he'll attend to you, take pride in you, do his best for you?
What I'm trying to do here is get you to relax, not be so preoccupied with getting so you can respond to God's giving.
People who don't know God and the way he works fuss over these things, but you know both God and how he works.
Steep yourself in God-reality, God-initiative, God-provisions.
You'll find all your everyday human concerns will be met.
Don't be afraid of missing out. You're my dearest friends!
The Father wants to give you the very kingdom itself.
Be generous. Give to the poor. Get yourselves a bank that can't go bankrupt, a bank in heaven far from bank robbers, safe from embezzlers, a bank you can bank on.
It's obvious, isn't it? The place where your treasure is,
is the place you will most want to be—and end up being."
Luke 12:22–34 (MSG)

Contentment Is The
Greatest Gain

Ecclesiastes 6:9 *"It is better to be happy with what you have than to always want more and more."* (ERV)

Now that's a refreshing scripture! We think getting *more* and *more* leads to happiness. But the truth is, it is better to be satisfied with what you have than to be always wanting *more*.

There's peace in "I have."
There's striving in "I want."

"I have" has already been achieved, "I want" comes with the burden of trying to obtain it.

"I have" is grounded in gratitude.

"I want" is rooted in lack.

"I have" recognizes blessing.

"I want" blinds us to what's already in our hands.

I have a home.
I have a family.
I have friends.
I have love.
I have a job.
I have clothes in my wardrobe and food in my pantry.
I have a car to drive, a bed to rest in, and the health to rise each morning.
I have laughter, memories, hope, faith, and a spirit from God.

I have all I truly need in this life to be content and fulfilled.
The only reason I wouldn't be content is if I get caught up in wanting more.

Why should I though? When I have *more* than enough.

When does enough become enough? When do we reach the point where we realise, we have been given more than enough? Considering a large majority of the world is lacking the basics, if you have food, clothing and shelter you are doing just fine.

Contentment doesn't come from getting more.
It comes from realizing that you already have enough.

How often do we pause to truly count our blessings?
When was the last time gratitude came up in your conversations with a friend?

I've noticed how often we speak from a place of longing.
"I want this."
"I can't wait to have that."
But rarely do we hear:

"I already have this."
"I'm so thankful for that."

Imagine if we shifted that narrative.
What if we started surprising people-not with complaints or wish lists-but with our gratitude?

It would be refreshing.
It would be contagious.
It could even change the atmosphere around us.

We have the power to pause the pursuit of what we think we lack, and to celebrate what we've already been given. The life we're chasing is already here, just waiting to be appreciated.

> But godliness with contentment is great gain. For we brought nothing into the world, and we can take nothing out of it. But if we have food and clothing, we will be content with that. Those who want to get rich fall into temptation and a trap and into many foolish and harmful desires that plunge people into ruin and destruction. For the love of money is a root of all kinds of evil. Some people, eager for money, have wandered from the faith and pierced themselves with many griefs.
> 1 Timothy 6:6 (NIV)

I'm not saying we shouldn't desire good or even great things in this life. On the contrary, the Bible has examples of God's people being blessed abundantly and becoming a blessing to the nations. There are also examples of God's people in seasons of lack. Neither is a sure sign of favour.

But seeking wealth separately from God by doing things our own way and bringing compromise into it is where trouble starts.

Many have sold their souls short in pursuit of wealth, and have paid dearly for it; mentally, physically, and spiritually.

Look at Judas Iscariot, the first disciple, who famously sold-out Jesus for thirty pieces of silver. His story ended in devastation; a man consumed by the torment of his soul. He tried to give the money back and undo his mistake. It was all too late. Jesus was on the cross and he was left hanging. The money he earned couldn't save his soul.

Jesus said,

> *What good will it be for someone to gain the whole world, yet forfeit their soul? Or what can anyone give in exchange for their soul?*
> Matthew 16:26 (NIV)

Some people become completely consumed by wanting what everyone else has, though this pursuit never truly nourishes their soul. They look at someone else's car or house or clothes and compare it to their own. Discontentment sets in and before they know it, they are on the hunt for upgrades to outdo or equal them. Maxing loans and credit cards, spending their savings excessively, working themselves to the bone.

No matter how hard they try to keep up, there is always someone else out there with bigger and better, so they'll never be satisfied. They wind up chasing mirages in the desert, running endlessly after illusions, all the while remaining thirsty.

It is better to be satisfied with what you have than to be always wanting something else.

Enjoy what you already have. Run your own race, stay in your lane, and you'll find deeper satisfaction than chasing "more" could ever offer.

Stop telling yourself you need more to be happy. Take a moment to look around. Chances are, you already have plenty.

Got a wardrobe full of clothes? Enjoy them. You don't need another outfit-you need contentment.

Be at peace with your home. It may not stand as tall as another's.
But within its walls is your warmth, your laughter, your life, and your light.
And while some chase more, others would give anything for what you have.
The world is full of homeless people who would love a house to call home.

A house is material; a home is the heart. Focus on building a home where your family wants to dwell in love, peace, and unity. Where there's fun, laughter, and good times. You can have the most expensive, beautiful mansions filled with the loneliest, most miserable, strife-ridden people. Have you ever walked into a house like that where you can feel the tension in the atmosphere? Would you want to live there?

But on the other hand, you can have a humble house that is so warm, inviting, and comfortable that no one wants to leave. You set the tone for your house. You create the energy and atmosphere. Good energy offers more than any designer couch or renovation could.

That's the power of atmosphere. That's the power of love. A power that *things* can't bring to the equation.

Why do we constantly compare ourselves to influencers or those who appear to have it all? Why envy someone when you don't truly know their story? You don't see their struggles, their pain, or the condition of their soul. What you admire on the surface may hide battles you can't even imagine. A flawless appearance means little if the soul is in turmoil.

Why stress over what others might think if you don't have the latest phone, car, or trending stuff. Your worth doesn't come from things-it comes from God. Maybe you've realized that chasing the latest craze isn't a good investment. Maybe you're wise enough to see beyond temporary trends. Maybe you're brave enough to wear those no-name shoes because you're saving for something that truly matters-like your future. Choose purpose over pressure. Choose lasting value over fleeting approval. Since when did our worth come from the labels we wear? They can wear their Gucci and Prada and break their bank balances. You can wear your smile and happy, friendly disposition.

> *Let God almighty be your gold and let him be your silver piled high for you. Then you will always trust in God and find that he is the source of your joy.* Job 22:25 (GNT)

If God is the source of our joy, why do we expect material things to be?

We live in a world of endless wants and excess, yet we never seem quite happy with the vast amounts we already have. When will we realise that *things* aren't doing it for us? When will we understand that our possessions aren't making us happy? In fact, they're weighing us down with their upkeep and making us slaves to work.

Things don't make us happy. They might bring a fleeting thrill in the moment of purchase, but once that wears off, so does the happiness. But a walk along the beach at sunset could. Some quiet time spent in prayer would. That hug from your loved one should. Playing sport with your besties could. There are so many ways to enjoy life - if we could let go of the constant urge to outdo each other with material things.

> *Tell those rich in this world's wealth to quit being so full of themselves and so obsessed with money, which is here today and gone tomorrow. Tell them to go after God, who piles on all the riches we could ever manage—to do good, to be rich in helping others, to be extravagantly generous. If they do that, they'll build a treasury that will last, gaining life that is truly life.* 1 Timothy 6:17-19 (MSG)

Why do we measure our worth by our riches, when one day we'll leave this life behind, and we can't take anything with us where we're going?

We are spiritual beings having an earthly experience that doesn't last forever. We sometimes live like it does.

What will we look like in eternity? Will there be physical distinctions among us? Or will we all look the same to even the playing field? I don't know, but I do know we'll leave this earthly face and body behind, and it will return to dust, ashes, and earth. Anything we have accumulated will be left behind for those who come after us to enjoy- and one day left to someone else we haven't even met. We will be remembered for a few generations, then long forgotten when no one's left on earth who knew us by name. They won't know if we wore designer clothes or lived in a luxurious house. How we impacted those around us, they'll never know. Were we good? Were we bad? Only God could keep such accounts.

I know the temporary physical realm seems so important right now, so we obsess over it and give it top priority. We build our kingdoms, groom our bodies, and work a third of our lifespans trying to obtain earthly things. There are winners and losers, rich and poor. The prideful, the humble. Those living in abundance, those living in scarcity.

The world is striving to be rich, despite Jesus saying, "Blessed are the poor." The world is striving to be wealthy, despite Jesus saying, "It's easier to gallop a camel through a needle's eye than for the rich to enter God's kingdom."

Jesus continued to say, "With God, all things are possible"- that's good news for the rich. Being rich is a challenge not everyone can conquer. Maybe it's a good thing not everyone is afforded the challenge.

The Bible says,

> *Those Christians who are poor must be glad when God lifts them up, and the rich Christians must be glad when God brings them down.* James 1:9 (GNT)

> *Happy are those who remain faithful under trials, because when they succeed in passing such a test, they will receive as their reward the life which God has promised to those who love him.* James 1:12 (GNT)

Our souls' progress and health are God's first and foremost concern, and both seasons will do their work for our souls if we let them.

We trust each season and let God do the work on our souls required. That's how I could lose half my earthly wealth at one stage of my life and keep smiling. My soul prospered even when my bank account declined.

The writer of proverbs once declared,

> *"Keep falsehood and lies far from me; give me neither poverty nor riches, but give me only my daily bread. Otherwise, I may have too much and disown you and say, 'Who is the Lord?' Or I may become poor and steal, and so dishonour the name of my God.* Proverbs 30:8 (NIV)

I don't think it's wrong to strive for financial abundance. There's no joy in stressing about where your next meal is coming from or how you will pay your bills. There is no glory in poverty and lack and not being able to fill your house with the groceries your family deserves and needs. Money can support so many good causes and is a useful resource for this earthly experience. But sometimes, the wealthier one becomes, the more they want, and the more out of touch with reality they become. The things they need just get more ludicrous. They once needed food, shelter, and good clothing- now they need a three million diamond-encrusted collar for their dog. Does the dog really care if it's wearing rubber, vinyl, or diamonds? To tell you the truth, it probably prefers leather - lightweight and comfortable.

That dog collar doesn't serve a purpose other than showing off one's wealth. But put that three million into a struggling single mums' bank account - well, her and her children will praise you and God forever. Even the thought makes me smile. That's providing for real needs. Lifting burdens, easing loads, and blessing humanity with your excess.

> *Our people must learn to spend their time doing good, in order to provide for real needs; they should not live useless lives.* Titus 3:14 (GNT)

In the light of eternity, our earthly financial pursuits will not be so important. That's good news for those not completely happy with their physical realm cards. It's a wake-up call for those that are.

When you find yourself in the hands of eternity, earthly currency doesn't count, and God's favour can't be bought with it.

> *For we brought nothing into the world, and we can take nothing out of it.* 1 Timothy 6:7 (NIV)

> *"Don't hoard treasure down here where it gets eaten by moths and corroded by rust or—worse! — stolen by burglars. Stockpile treasure in heaven, where it's safe from moth and rust and burglars. It's obvious, isn't it? The place where your treasure is, is the place you will want to be, and end up being.* Matthew 6:19 (MSG)

I once naively believed that my lack of worldly fame and success was God forgetting to favour me. I wanted to be rich, I wanted to be famous. I even wrote a song about it.

I thought if I prayed harder, worked smarter, and did all the things good girls should do, such as attend church, believe, and refrain from sin, I would be rewarded with huge financial blessings and earthly success.

Now I simply trust that *"blessed are the poor,"* and that's why God has kept me exactly where I need to be for my soul's progress, happiness, and evolution. Contentment with godliness is great gain. Saints are known to God, and that is enough.

If my true rewards are in eternity why blame God for not giving them to me fully yet?

> *When you grab all you can get, that's what happens: the more you get, the less you are.* Proverbs 1:19 (MSG)

I want more in other ways now. More life. More of God. More time. More love. More family moments, More freedom. Not more things.

> *Why is everyone hungry for more? "More, more," they say. "More, more." I have God's more-than-enough. More joy in one ordinary day than they get in all their shopping sprees. At day's end I'm ready for sound sleep, for you, God, have put my life back together.* Psalm 4:6 (MSG)

Tending To The
Real World

If the Internet crashed tomorrow, and there was no more Instagram, Facebook, TikTok, YouTube, or AI?
What would your life look like?
Would you still have a life?

When my daughter was little, I boycotted social media. No Facebook, no Instagram, no endless scrolling. All the sites that I thought may consume my time and take priceless moments away from me and my little one. I didn't want to tend to an online world while the real one was right in front of me, needing my full attention.

It may have been extreme, but I figured one day in my old age, my Instagram followers weren't going to take me grocery shopping when I could no longer drive or hang my clothes out to dry. I didn't have the time or energy to tend to both worlds, so one had to go.

The bond I built with my daughter during that season was priceless. I have no regrets. I hope she will remember me as the mum whose eyes were on her and not glued to a screen. Even now, when I feel my phone creeping back in to steal more of my time, the rebel in me wants to throw caution to the wind and let my phone battery die for a few weeks just to get a break from the constant onslaught. Wouldn't it be nice if people *couldn't* reach you for a bit? I grew up without a phone, and I remember how *liberating* that was.

These days, though, it's harder. Life demands our phones. Schools, employers, sporting schedules, emails, rosters, bills, business, and social media all have their pull on us. All vying for our attention and able to disrupt us at any given moment as we carry around these smartphones. It's draining our batteries without us even knowing it.

Not long ago, we went camping with my family. Out in the bush, there was no phone reception. At first, it felt like a challenge- but the rewards were greater than I could have imagined. Without screens, everyone was present. Really present.

It was a joy to watch life unfold without technology tugging at our attention. The kids played in the park, swam in the lake, and dealt cards for endless rounds of Uno. They helped with dinner, roasted marshmallows, and carried on lively conversations with us adults. The teens stepped out from the shells that technology so often builds around them. When a phone is in reach, they don't always notice the world right in front of them or give us their time. But without it, they are with us fully. We get them back.

It was beautiful to see. Even more beautiful to feel.

But soon, we returned home- and the screens returned with us. Nature and real-life company had done wonders for our souls, yet it's so easy to slip back into habits. I wish I knew how to keep this simplicity close. It's hard when life demands its digital use.

I wish our voices shaped our children's hearts more than their phones did. I don't know what the phone whispers to my daughter- but I know what I would say.

The online world can be fake and fickle. So much of it seems like a competition- who is the most popular, who has the most followers, who is the prettiest, fittest, slimmest, and sexiest. I'm happy to give everyone their titles though. Be the prettiest. Be the most popular. Be the sexiest. I'm happy for others to shine and be successful and fill their cups.

But lately, I've been wondering...
Where are the people competing for titles that matter?

Like, who is the kindest?
The most caring?
The most generous?
The most loving?
Who is leaving the greatest positive impact on the world?

Did Mother Teresa have a TikTok account? Probably not. She was tending to *the real world*. What a legacy she left by doing so. You can achieve some amazing things when you get rid of distractions, stop chasing digital applause and start tending to the real world.

The things that used to impress, don't impress me anymore. Posting a picture of a million-dollar car and a luxurious lifestyle was once impressive and all, but what would be *truly* impressive is if the 10% of people holding 85% of the world's wealth sold off a few of their excess toys and gave the proceeds to the millions of families who could truly use that support to live.

To put food on the table for their families. To pay for their electricity or medical needs. I would *definitely* go out of my way to like and share that.

According to Wikipedia, 1% of the world's population controls about 40% of its wealth, while the bottom 50% share just 2%.

I'm not Mother Teresa. I'm not courageous enough to sell all my earthly belongings to give to the poor. But I *can* do something. I *have* something to give that could ease some of the suffering. Even a 1% donation. If we all did a little something, it would add up to something big.

We could all make our presence count for more. The world could be blessed because we were in it.

We're trying to find life and connection through our phones, but nothing can compare to real life, real connections and making a positive difference.

If we put down our phones for a bit and got out in the real world, no doubt we would find this connection. We would find a passion and a purpose to serve. We would see the difference we could make in our communities. We could live and connect without a phone attached to our fingertips.

Why neglect the real world for a counterfeit?

Technology is great. But humankind is greater.

No one wants to get to the end of their life and wish they had lived more, scrolled less, and supported better causes.

I'm sure we can leave the world a little better than we found it.

"This is a large work I've called you into, but don't be overwhelmed. It's best to start small. Give a cool cup of water to someone who is thirsty, for instance. The smallest act of giving or receiving makes you my apprentice. You won't miss out on a thing." Matthew 10:41 (MSG)

Things They *Said* Would Come

In a distant land, over two thousand years ago, the Apostle Paul wrote to a young man named Timothy, warning him of things to come. The words become part of the New Testament in the Bible.

Paul wrote:

> *You should know this, Timothy, that in the last days there will be very difficult times. For people will love only themselves and their money. They will be boastful and proud, scoffing at God, disobedient to their parents, and ungrateful. They will consider nothing sacred. They will be unloving and unforgiving; they will slander others and have no self-control. They will be cruel and hate what is good. They will betray friends, be reckless, be puffed up with pride, and love pleasure rather than God. They will act religious, but they will reject the power of God that could make them godly.* 2 Timothy 3:1-5 (NLT)

Two thousand years later-

The world looks startlingly familiar to what was described.

Doesn't this sum up the world around us?

Isn't this the norm we've grown accustomed to seeing every day?

Have you not seen it? People being boastful and proud, unloving and unforgiving. People betraying friends, and being reckless? People loving pleasure, rather than God. Or acting like they serve God but lacking the power of God that could make them godly?

This, of course, is our norm.
But two thousand years ago, it was a far-fetched notion. A wild claim. A prediction that seemed impossible.

Yet here we are.
The prophecy has come to life.
The Apostle's words have proven true and accurate.

If we have arrived at that moment, are these the end times? Should we be packing our bags for eternity, or at least preparing to?

If the curtain is about to fall on this earthly stage, are we the most unprepared generation for an encounter with God?

The bible says that day would come like a thief in the night.
That we'd be eating, drinking, marrying, going about our lives-completely unaware of what was coming.
And then, suddenly, it will be over.

The shock of it.
The tears.

The regret.

We thought we had forever. An endless array of time. But we didn't.

The game of life's over and we've just realized we didn't play it that well.

Like the rich man in Jesus parable (Luke 16:19-31) who lived in comfort while ignoring poor Lazarus at his gate.
When the rich man died, he wanted a second chance.
He begged to return, to warn his brothers. To warn them to live better and do better.
But it was too late.

It is all too late when our day on earth is over. We can't come back and live it better.

Thank God we still have today to play a better game.

To *not let that day catch us unaware,* like Jesus declared.

Even if the earth endures forever, our bodies won't.
Our time on earth has an end.

We can spend decades building our kingdoms on earth and beautifying our worlds and miss the whole point of this earthly experience.

If we could go back in time and tell the early believers how we live today, what might they think? Would they marvel at our progress- or be puzzled by our priorities? Would our overflowing closets and walk-in wardrobes seem like abundance- or confusion? Would our malls filled with endless choices delight them- or overwhelm them?

"Wow," they might say, "What a wealthy world! Has poverty been eliminated?"

And we'd have to reply-if we're even aware-
"No. Nearly 9 million people still die of hunger and malnutrition every year.

How would we explain this? The two extremes.
How would we justify some earning millions by the hour and living in excess, while others starve to death?

I don't think we want to be the generation remembered for excess and emptiness. We are just under pressure. The pressure is relentless. It comes at us constantly in many ways. It tells us we're not enough-so we strive to be. The struggle is real. We're just trying to survive in a world that tells us we must hustle for our worth. That without things we're not enough.

We're trying to survive in other ways. To stay relevant, to stay liked, to stay loved. This difficult world is hard to please.

But we're not here to gain worldly approval. We're not here to be slaves to investments, fashion, and materialism. Should we let society dictate our worth based on our looks, the house we own, or the clothes we wear? Should we jump through ridiculous hoops to be loved and accepted and popular?

Are we not enough just as we are?

Should we spend countless hours in a workplace sacrificing our precious invaluable time, just to waste our paychecks on things that won't ultimately add value to our lives or futures, to try to stop tongues that will wag regardless?

Things have never cured anyone of depression.
But there have been plenty of people transformed inwardly by the power of God and living for a higher cause.

> *Has anyone by fussing in front of the mirror ever gotten taller by so much as an inch? All this time and money wasted on fashion—do you think it makes that much difference? Instead of looking at the fashions, walk out into the fields and look at the wildflowers. They never primp or shop, but have you ever seen color and design quite like it? The ten best-dressed men and women in the country look shabby alongside them. If God gives such attention to the appearance of wildflowers—most of which are never seen— don't you think he'll attend to you, take pride in you, do his best for you? What I'm trying to do here is to get you to relax, to not be so preoccupied with getting, so you can respond to God's giving.* Matthew 6:27 (MSG)

Maybe we can't change the whole world.
Maybe we're not supposed to.
God knows our pressures. The high cost of living. Our personal responsibilities.

But we *can* bless our homes.
Our streets.
Our neighbourhoods.
Our families.

We can make a positive difference right where we are. We can raise good children, modelling morals, kindness and good values. We could offer someone a meal, a kind word, or a cup of cold water. We could reach out to our disadvantaged communities.

If each of us lit a little light in our corner of the world.
Wouldn't the world be brighter? Lazarus wasn't asking the rich man for much.
Just a few leftovers from his table. I'm sure we've got some leftovers to give.

> *Therefore, as we have opportunity, let us do good to all people, especially to those who belong to the family of believers.*
> Galatians 6:10 (NIV)

Creating

If you're a believer and you've read Genesis in the Bible, you'll know creativity started with God.

In the beginning, the world was formless, empty, and dark. And then, God began to create. Creation.

Life.

Light.

God turned darkness into light. Formed the seas and skies. Brought forth wildlife and nature — all the incredible, awe-inspiring things around us. Things I believe are far too magnificent and intricately designed to be the result of mere accident or coincidence.

Then, God created humankind in His own image.
And God's very first commandment to humankind was:

> *"Prosper! Reproduce! Fill earth! Take charge! Be responsible for fish in the sea and birds in the air, for every living thing that moves on the face of Earth."* Genesis 1:28 (NLT)

So we did. Like our Creator, humans began creating too. The impulse to build, design, and innovate was woven into our DNA; powered by that first command.

Everything we see today exists because creation kept on creating. Over time, humanity discovered electricity, transportation, technology, flight, artificial intelligence — and the list continues to grow. Every year, thousands of new products emerge as creativity continues to thrive.

From the very beginning, everything we needed to create was already here, woven into nature, waiting to be uncovered. These creations were invisible, hidden in the soil, in the trees, in the rocks. But over time, creations have emerged, brought to life by visionary minds.

Humanity has achieved extraordinary things, leaving legacies that have advanced humankind.

You really can start with nothing and create something wonderful — using creative eyes.

Some creations are deemed more important than others, but I can't live without my potato peeler—so I say they all matter and have their place.

And good news is, there's still room for more. Your creation.

Creating takes courage, determination, belief and a whole lot of resilience. Not everyone will see your vision. Not all projects will succeed — some are just test runs.

There will be doubters, naysayers, even haters.
Progress always meets some form of resistance.

The challenge is to create anyway. Your unique piece.
To keep going. Undaunted. Unshaken. Belief intact.

You are here for a reason.
To do the creative best you can with the life you've been given. To *'Prosper!*
Reproduce! Fill earth! Take charge!'
And you should absolutely, unapologetically, do just that.

> *Please don't squander one bit of this marvelous life God has*
> *given us.* 2 Corinthians 6:1 (MSG)

A Case Of Stolen
Potential

I still remember the day vividly. I was crying in the church toilets, begging my mum to take me home, adamant that I wasn't going on stage to sing.

A ten-year-old girl, deeply hurt by cruel and nasty comments that had found their way to my ears during rehearsal.

I practised for weeks. Been so excited to be singing the solo in the church choir before the entire congregation. My dad was coming to watch and he *never* went to church or watched.

But now, the excitement had turned to tears.

To this day, I don't remember exactly what was said, but I know it was something nasty and negative about my singing abilities, said with a smirk and a giggle by two other girls.

It was enough to knock me off my perch and rattle my insecurities. The show wouldn't go on, and neither would I.

I'm not sure what my mum said to me in that moment. Whatever it was, it worked. Just enough to get me on that stage and the solo sung. Yes, I sang. I took my place. But even then, I only walked away with the negatives. No matter how many positive comments came my way afterwards, the damage had already been done. The negatives screamed much louder. That was my first and last solo.

Fast forward twenty-five years. Twenty-five years of soul-searching and personal development of growth and maturity. Twenty-five years of self-help, divine intervention, and lived experience. I was now a thirty-five-year-old woman and mother - nothing like the shy, inhibited, and insecure ten-year-old I once was.

I was strong now in so many areas, though I still didn't sing solos.

One day, a lady approached me after a church service and said, "I know who you are!"

"I have footage of you singing a church solo from my daughter's christening when you were a child."

I cringed. Great, I thought. Destroy it.

The following week, she brought me a USB with that fateful moment. The day I'd made my singing debut. The day I learned "I wasn't good enough." The day I let someone else's smirks and whispers shrink me. The world would've laughed too, had I pursued singing further.

I took it home and watched. I took it home and rewatched.

I was pleasantly surprised!

"That was pretty darn good for a ten-year-old," I thought. Nothing like the disaster my mind had re-enacted over the years. I was genuinely proud of my efforts.

Okay, I was no child singing prodigy, but I wasn't a flop either. It was a million times better than my mind had remembered.

With mature eyes, I saw a completely different story. I saw a beautiful, sweet, innocent girl singing with a lovely, gentle, pure voice.

I wanted to speak to my ten-year-old self now. I wanted to say, "Why were you crying in a toilet when you should have been standing tall? Why did you believe the jealous girls instead of believing in yourself and your God?" I wanted to nurture the girl others had hurt. Encourage her where others had discouraged.

I wondered how my life would have played out differently if I had never taken their words to heart. Because I would have lived life a little differently, I was sure. Maybe I would have joined the school choir like my heart wanted to. Maybe I would have auditioned for that musical. Maybe I would have started a band or gotten some lessons and perfected my craft. Instead, I did nothing. I never sang again. A seedling lost to nasty weeds.

I was upset now, but for different reasons. I was upset because of stolen opportunities and lost dreams. For years of doubt and discouragement where they need only have been hope and dreams.

I was sad that I hadn't been strong enough to weather that storm. I didn't need to be the best, nor have the best voice. I just needed belief! Belief that I could do it regardless. I wanted to scream now: "JUST KEEP SINGING!" I longed to redeem that moment. I still do.

I can't go back. Life is not a choose-your-own-adventure book that we get to do over to make better choices. Life doesn't work that way. But I can tell you. You, who might be at the beginning of your journey: don't let anyone convince you, you can't dream. The only person who truly needs to believe in the potential of your dreams is you. You are the author and finisher of your dream. The one called to fulfill them. The only person who truly can.

> *"This is what I do: I don't look back, I lengthen my stride, and I run straight towards the goal to win the prize that Gods heavenly call offers."* Philippians 3:13 (GW)

It's never too late to pick up a dream or two. To reclaim potential. To pivot back to your heart's desires and first loves. To try again and lengthen your stride. To pick up the pen. Or the mic. Or the paint brush. Or whatever craft you've left behind, that you thought you weren't good enough for. You can always revisit that thing you thought you weren't "good enough" for.

Who said you had to be 'good enough'? Who said only the best singers get to sing? Who said only the best writers get to write? Only the perfect deserve a platform? Who said it needed to be perfect, or amazing or outstanding? Is it not enough to be uniquely yours?

Creators simply create.

Some will like it. Some will hate it. Who cares if you're bringing your unique piece to the table and enjoying the gift you've been given.

"Use what talents you possess; the woods would be very silent if no birds sang there except those that sang best."
Henry van Dyke

So now, I bring my unique sound, regardless. Some may like it. Some may loathe it.

I know it's not extraordinary.
But it's simply me.
And being simply me is all I'm called to be.

Sorry, haters - I'll sing again, even with an ordinary voice.
Sorry, doubters - I'll write again, even with my ordinary words.
I'll make my music. I'll tell my tales.
I'll sow my seeds. I'll bring my piece.

It makes me happy. It brings me joy.
If happiness is all I get from it, then that is enough.
What price would you pay for happiness?

When I leave this earth, I will have left something behind.
And that's all I can do.
What happens after that is out of my control.
It is enough to have planted my seed.
Nature and God do the rest.

What if those who have already left this earth didn't bring their songs? What if they took them to the grave? Would we still be in darkness? Would we lack flight? Would technology be half what it is? Would disease and sickness be rifer? Would we be as advanced, inspired, or connected?

The world is what it is - and isn't - due to people bringing their song or not bringing their song.

Whether your song is being a great parent, writing a book, blessing your community, building a business, or creating something entirely new-why shouldn't you bring it, just because some people say it's not good enough?

Some artists are never recognized in their time.
Some are overlooked, ridiculed, even crucified.
Yet generations later, they're celebrated.

Do we need the accolade in our lifetime, or do we plant our seeds for the future generations regardless?

Have you ever finished a puzzle only to find a piece missing?
That's your piece if you don't bring it.

Who cares if it's an amazing piece or an ordinary piece?
Bring it anyway. It's part of earth's puzzle and is needed for the overall picture.

In nature, mango trees don't withhold fruit just because some people hate mangoes.
They bear fruit-and those who love mangoes rejoice.
God didn't create the mango tree for the mango haters.
God created the mango tree for the mango lovers.

So, keep bearing your fruit.
Keep being who you were created to be.
Keep producing what you were created to produce.

Because someone out there will love what you create.

You aren't here by chance. You're here for a creative purpose. For experience and adventure. To grow and evolve and be your own type of unique and wonderful.

Whatever you are here to do, let it be done in your lifetime.
Embrace everything that makes you, *you*-even the weaker parts.
There is a place for every person, every gift, and every voice in the choir of earth.

You were born to be a blessing. Be that.

Earth is a battle between darkness and light. The unseen spiritual forces of good versus evil.

Be the light. Be the good.

> *The light shines in the darkness, and the darkness has never put it out.* John 1:5 (GNT)

> *"God in his kindness gave each of us different gifts."* Romans 12:6 (GW)

> *Each of you as a good manager must use the gift that God has given you to serve others.* 1 Peter 4:10 (GW)

The Lords *Prayer*

Jesus once taught us to pray this pray:

> *"Our Father in heaven: May your holy name be honoured; may your Kingdom come; may your will be done on earth as it is in heaven. Give us today the food we need. Forgive us the wrongs we have done, as we forgive the wrongs that others have done to us. Do not bring us to hard testing but keep us safe from the Evil one."* Matthew 6:9-13 (GNT)

If God's will *were* truly being done on earth as it is in heaven, Jesus wouldn't have come to earth to make changes.

He would have come into the world, found everything in order, and would not have needed to influence it in any way. He would have declared 'God was in control of all that was happening, and everything was A-OK.' Jesus would have simply sat back, relaxed, and preached a different message. The message would be, *"Everything is as it should be, and God's will is already being done."*

But that's not what Jesus did.

He came to earth on a mission to set things right. He stepped into a broken world and opened the eyes of the blind — *God didn't want them blind.*
He came into the world and healed the sick — *God didn't want them sick.*
He raised the dead — *God didn't want them to die prematurely.*
He preached good news and provided for the poor — *God didn't want them poor and misinformed.*
He loved the downcast and rejected — *God didn't want them downcast and rejected, overlooked or cast aside..*

Jesus even challenged the church, the religious establishment of the day. The very place where you'd expect God's will to be done. The very place you'd expect to find God's will alive and active. He found it corrupted.
So, Jesus spoke truth.
He cast out afflictions.
He comforted the sorrowful.
He overturned tables.
He walked with the weak.

That's what God's will looks like in action: love, truth, compassion, care, empathy, healing, life, and equality. All played out in Jesus' ministry.
Greater things we were told to do, though I haven't seen them yet.

Jesus said, *"The thief comes only in order to steal, kill, and destroy. I have come in order that you might have life- life in all its fullness."* John 10:10 (GNT)

That was God's will and God's mission for Jesus — to bring heaven's will to earth and to show us what it looks like when God reigns.
It looks a lot like Love.

If God's will *were* already being done on earth, Jesus wouldn't have taught us to pray, *"Your kingdom come, your will be done on earth as it is in heaven"* (Matthew 6:9–10).
Instead, he would have said, *"Thank you, God, that no matter what we face, your perfect will is always being done here on earth, just like it is in heaven."*

I just wanted to clear that up in case you're blaming God for everything.

Jesus said we are God's hands and feet on this earth — the salt of the earth. So if the world is tasteless, saltless, sour, bitter, or broken. I guess we can point the finger at ourselves.

God didn't create the mess. We did.

By our decisions, by our actions, by our thoughts.

We are the inhabitants and caretakers of this world.
We have the power to make it beautiful-or not so.
We can bring flavour and light into every space we enter.
Our homes, our workplaces, our churches, our communities.

A church is only as good as the spirit in it.
So is a community.
So is a nation.
So is the world.

Jesus said it plainly in Matthew 5:13 (MSG):

> *"Let me tell you why you are here. You're here to be salt-seasoning that brings out the God-flavors of this earth. If you lose your saltiness, how will people taste godliness?"*

It's a huge injustice when we blame God for the problems of the world. When God created us to be the solution.

If the world is saltless, maybe it's because we are.

> *Remain in me, as I also remain in you. No branch can bear fruit by itself; it must remain in the vine. Neither can you bear fruit unless you remain in me.* John 15:4 (NIV)

The God Of Ordinary A
Extraordinary Things

If God was just a God of extraordinary things, then Jesus would never have been born in a stable. A palace would have been a more suitable place for the Son of God to arrive. Maybe a gold-plated crib, a queen for a mother, or some other wealthy benefactor. Why did Jesus even need a mother? Couldn't the heavens have simply opened, with God's hand reaching down planting his son on earth?

Why the rough donkey ride entrance into a little-known town called Bethlehem? To little unknown parents?

God revealed the news of Jesus to wealthy wise men carrying treasures-but He also entrusted it to poor shepherds, the social outcasts of the day. And they, not the religious elite, were given first visiting rights to the newborn King.

Why did unclean, unimportant shepherds get first visiting rights - the front-row seats to history? You'd expect the choir of angels to inform the priests, religious leaders of the day, the squeaky clean, the prophets, those following the holy rules, the rich, the powerful. But instead, the angels filled the sky with hallelujahs for a handful of humble shepherds.

When the angels proclaimed, "good news to all people," that's exactly what they meant- to all people! Lowly shepherds included.

God chose ordinary, everyday people.

Hallelujah for the shepherds and the rest of us ordinary people. The good news was for one and all.

God is the God of extraordinary things and ordinary things.

If God was just a God of extraordinary things, the twelve disciples would never have been chosen. There were scholars in town - Pharisees and Sadducees - those who knew the scriptures like the back of their hands. Surely they were the obvious choice. If there had been a recruitment process and résumés submitted, the twelve disciples wouldn't have made the first cut. Fishermen. Tradesmen. The Uneducated. Hardly the ideal candidates to carry out an important mission to save the world. Hardly the people you would expect, to be disciples of a spiritual Son of God, with a righteous kingdom to build. Yet they were the ones Jesus deliberately called and chose.

God is the God of the educated and the uneducated.

If God was just a God of extraordinary things, then surely the prophets who spoke in God's name would have lived in abundance. After all, some of them stopped the rain, called down fire from heaven and silenced kings.

Surely, they wouldn't need help from a poor widow to fund their mission-like the prophet Elijah did. That shouldn't happen, right?

Wasn't God supposed to provide ten thousand cattle on a hill for his people? Overflowing their pockets with provisions? That's what prosperity preachers tell us.

God worked miracles through Elijah. Kings honoured him, and others feared him. But at one point, he turned to a widow for her last meal. Shouldn't he be asking the king or some other nobility to fund his cause? Instead, God purposely sent him to a widow. A widow, with nothing but a handful of flour and a drop of oil. The unlikely choice for provision and salvation.

But in God's hands, that small offering created endless supply and a miracle.

God is the God of the strong and the weak.

Scripture gives plenty of examples where God partners with the poor, the weak, the outcast, and the rejected. So why do we often believe God is only present in abundance. That wealth and success equals God's favour.

On the contrary, Jesus said, *"Blessed are the poor in spirit, for theirs is the kingdom of heaven."*

I am glad that God opens the kingdom of heaven to all people-not just the rich, prosperous, successful VIPs driving luxury cars and wearing designer clothes.

God is the God of the rich and the poor

We came into the world naked, and we'll leave it the same way. God doesn't measure success by scales that are temporary. God is looking for love, joy, peace, patience, kindness, goodness, humility, faithfulness, gentleness, and self-control. Not fat bank accounts or social status. I guess these are the things that last in our hearts and spirit when everything else fades away.

> *Do not love this world nor the things it offers you, for when you love the world, you do not have the love of the Father in you. For the world offers only a craving for physical pleasure, a craving for everything we see, and pride in our achievements and possessions. The world and its desires pass away, but whoever does the will of God lives forever.* 1 John 2:15 (NLT)

Life is beautiful, and it's here to be enjoyed. Just remember there is an eternal kingdom while you are building your temporary earthly one.

> *Each one of these people of faith died not yet having in hand what was promised, but still believing. How did they do it? They saw it way off in the distance, waved their greeting, and accepted the fact that they were transients in this world. People who live this way make it plain that they are looking for their true home. If they were homesick for the old country, they could have gone back any time they wanted. But they were after a far better country than that- heaven country. You can see why God is so proud of them, and has a City waiting for them.* Hebrews 11:13-16 (MSG)

Being rich isn't a sign of God's favour. Nor is being poor. But there are far better things to pursue in life than money. Like love, purpose, health, joy, and peace. That's the true path to a richer life.

What can we bring to the table that's truly valuable? Our joyful, happy, peaceful disposition. Our wisdom and emotional IQ. And this makes others far happier than our designer jacket or riches ever could.

> *I have learned to be satisfied with what I have. I know what it is to be in need and what it is to have more than enough. I have learned this secret, so that anywhere, at any time, I am content, whether I am full or hungry, whether I have too much or too little. I have the strength to face all conditions by the power Christ gives me.* Philippians 4:11-13 (GNT)

> *Don't be obsessed with getting more material things. Be relaxed with what you have. Since God assured us, "I'll never let you down, never walk off and leave you," we can boldly quote, God is there, ready to help; I'm fearless no matter what. Who or what can get to me?* Hebrews 13:5 (MSG)

Bearing *Fruit*

———— ⁓ ————

The thing about your fruit is…
People around you eat it.
So be mindful of what you are feeding them.

> *"But the Holy Spirit produces this kind of fruit in our lives: love, joy, peace, patience, kindness, goodness, faithfulness, gentleness, and self-control."* Galatians 5:22-23 (NLT)

It's not all about what you do.
(Though religious people might think it is)

It's not just about *doing.*
It's about *being.*
It's about *who you are being and becoming.*

It's about whether your life reflects the fruit of God's Spirit.

Jesus said it wouldn't profit a man to gain the whole world if he lost his soul in the process.

He said we would know His followers-
Not by their titles.
Not by their platforms.
But by their fruit.
The fruit of love.

The Bible says- Even if you have faith that moves mountains.
Even if you speak mightily in God's name.
Even if you give all your belongings to the poor or surrender your body to
the flames.
If you have not love,
You have gained *nothing*. (1 Corinthians 13:1)

Even if you are a priest and stand in a pulpit.
If you don't carry the heart of God in how you live,
The title means nothing and credits you nothing.

You can't call yourself a follower of God
And then harm your neighbour (a child of God.)
You can't follow God
And lie, cheat, abuse, or condemn your fellow man.

Jesus didn't do any of those things.
He *saved.*
He *uplifted.*
He *healed.*
He *helped.*
He *loved.*
He *forgave.*
He *provided.*

He *enlightened.*
He *set free.*

Shouldn't His followers do the same?

You can't claim to represent a political party but follow the principles of the opposition party, can you?

We've all seen the casualties of misguided faith—the extremes some pursue in God's name. It has rattled the world at times, bringing fear, destruction, and terror. If they have not loved they have gained *nothing.*

Can *that* kind of faith save them?

The Bible says,
"Faith without works is dead."
Faith without fruit is fake.

True faith saves your soul
Not just your image.

> *If I speak with human eloquence and angelic ecstasy but don't love, I'm nothing but the creaking of a rusty gate. If I speak God's word with power, revealing all his mysteries and making everything plain as day, and if I have faith that says to a mountain, "Jump," and it jumps, but I don't love, I'm nothing. If I give everything I own to the poor and even go to the stake to be burned as a martyr, but I don't love, I've gotten nowhere. So, no matter what I say, what I believe, and what I do, I'm bankrupt without love.* 1 Corinthians 13:1-7 (MSG)

"If you have love for one another, then everyone will know that you are my disciples." John 13:35 (GNT)

None of us have arrived yet.
It is a work in progress. This is a journey.
A pilgrimage.

We are all still becoming.

But love is what we should strive for. God can fill us with this love. If you're lacking, ask!

What the world needs now is love. Pure love.
What our families need now is love. Pure love.
What the communities around us need now is love. Pure love.

Where is this fruit of love?
Can the real disciples please stand up?

Religion

I grew up in a Christian household, and like anyone, I've fallen short of the rules that shaped my faith. I still fall short at times, yet grace always brings me back to God and faith.

I could claim the 'And still' motto like a true UFC champ:
And still, I follow God. Still loyal. Still steadfast. Still standing, despite the losses and the bruises and the failures.

I've come to see that it was never about rules. Faith isn't a black and white sketch; it's a canvas God keeps filling with colour. Religion often tries to contain, limit and control. I don't think that was ever God's intention for our spirits. Not when Jesus said He came to give us life to the full.
I also haven't forgotten who crucified Jesus for breaking man-made rules. The sinners didn't hang Jesus on a cross-the religious leaders did.

I reference Scripture because it has shaped me. But I know faith is a choice, not something to be forced on anyone. *Cultivate your own relationship with God, but don't impose it on others.* Romans 14:22 (MSG)

I'm still learning. Still evolving. And none of us have all the answers this side of eternity. Especially not me.

I leave salvation and revelation to God. That job's far too great for me. I continue to pray for God's will to be done, *starting in me.* That's all I can do. I think it's all I'm called to do. Be who God created me to be.

I believe God created human beings and relationships and it was a perfect idea in a perfect world. It's a legacy to last a lifetime with someone. To build a kingdom and fill it with loved ones. To watch it grow from strength to strength. It's a sight to behold.

When kingdoms crumble, as they sometimes do, you can still build a beautiful legacy though. Many have. Many still do.

> *Then the Lord God said, 'It is not good for the man to live alone. I will make a suitable companion to help him.' So he took some soil from the ground and formed all the animals and all the birds. Then he brought them to the man to see what he would name them; and that is how they got all their names. So the man named all the birds and all the animals; but none of them was a suitable companion to help him. Then the Lord God made the man fall into a deep sleep, and while he was sleeping, he took out one of the man's ribs and closed up the flesh. He formed a woman out of the rib and brought her to him. Then the man said, "At last, here is one of my own kind- Bone taken from my bone, and flesh from my flesh. 'Woman' is her name because she was taken out of a man." That is why man leaves his father and mother and is united with his wife, and they become one. The man and the woman were both naked, but they were not embarrassed.*
> Genesis 2:18-25 (GNT)

It can't get simpler than that

Adam needed a suitable companion. God made him one.
The man said:
"At last."

Bone of my bone. Flesh of my flesh.
They became one.
Oh and they were naked, and not ashamed.

I believe God doesn't just want us to live a holy life. God wants us to live
a passionate life. A vibrant life. A joyful life. A beautiful life. Exhilarating.
Adventurous.
I'm grateful God is a God of variety, colour and brilliance.

The earth is a marketplace of variety. Bursting with beauty. People don't all
look like us, live like us, believe like us or act like us. And that's okay.
We extend grace to one another.
We are called to love the whole fruit basket, to embrace every kind of fruit
— even the ones we don't prefer or fully understand.

> *But that doesn't mean you should all look and speak and act*
> *the same. Out of the generosity of Christ, each of us is given*
> *our own gift.* Ephesians 4:7 (MSG)

Jesus said God alone is judge. So why take God's place?

To judge a soul, you'd need all the facts: their full story, from birth until now.
Every moment. Every wound. Every influence. Their DNA, upbringing,
genes, culture, trauma. It's impossibly complex. Far too intricate to fathom.

Only God sees it all. Only God is righteous enough to weigh it. I leave the task to God. It's far too great a decision for me to make.

It's baffling when we think we can make such a judgement call based on first appearances and odd encounters.

We don't have all the answers to what is wrong or what is right. We're not supposed to. We weren't supposed to know right from wrong in the first place. Until someone ate an apple.

Maybe we should go back to innocence.
Lay down our rules and surrender to love. Hand back the apple and all it entailed.

Yes, sin can separate us from God. But only if our conscience lets it.
God is still waiting with open arms either way. If you ask the Prodigal Son and believe the parable.

My daughter didn't know right from wrong when she was young. She just knew where love lived. Love lived on my lap. And no matter what she did, she found her way back to it. She still does.

Jesus said,

> *you know how to give good gifts to your children. So how much more will your Father in heaven give good things to those who ask him?* Matthew 7:11 (GW)

> *Whenever our conscience condemns us, we will be reassured that God is greater than our conscience.* 1 John 3:20 (GW)

Whoever comes to me I will never drive away.
John 6:37 (NIV)

It's good to know you will never be turned away.
You can come, just as you are.
Pray. Learn. Ask. Trust.
You don't have to be good enough to come.
God said simply '*come.*'

The Bible wasn't written to bring death. It was written to bring life.
I believe God loves all His creations-even when His followers say some aren't worthy of that love.

We are all loved, regardless, by a God who is love. This I truly believe.

If there's any inner work to be done on a soul, God can handle it, without our interference.

> *Do you have any business crossing people off the guest list or interfering with God's welcome? If there are corrections to be made, God can handle that without your help.*
> Romans 14:2 (MSG)

There's a moment in Matthew's Gospel where mothers were trying to bring their children to Jesus for a blessing. Jesus' disciples were shooing them away. Denying them access.

The future King had more worthy things to attend to, they must have thought.

When Jesus found out people were being turned away, he was livid. Furious.

"Let the children come," He said. So he could bless them.
"The Kingdom belongs to such as these."

I don't think Jesus would stop at children.

"Let everyone come," Jesus would declare. You they them.

> *"Come to me, all you who are weary and burdened, and I will give you rest. Take my yoke upon you and learn from me, for I am gentle and humble in heart, and you will find rest for your souls. For my yoke is easy and my burden is light.*
> Matthew 11:28 (NIV)

Jesus declared His yoke is easy and His burden is light.
Remember that when some try to make the road heavy, burdened, and difficult.

The gospel is inclusive.
Even when disciples say it isn't.
Even when they build gates and walls God never asked for.

Not that long ago, left-handed children were being slapped for not writing with their right hand.
The ideology seems ludicrous now that things have changed and there is scientific evidence backing left-handed people. We don't slap left-handed children anymore.
We've learned.
We've adapted. We've accepted.

They were not evil. They didn't need punishment. It was not wrong to be left-handed. They are as equal as right-handed people, though once they weren't.

I pray we keep evolving in other areas where we remain ignorant.

We weren't made to be perfect.
If we were, we would probably worship ourselves.
God is the perfecter.
God is the finisher.
To God be the glory.

Let us adore Him and not ourselves and just live our lives the best we can, as loved and flawed humans.

I am unashamedly flawed but unapologetically loved.

I'm glad God loves me, just the way I am.
No matter what I do.
The Bible tells me so.
God loves you too.

I once renovated an old house. It was old and dirty but had the potential to be beautiful.
So every day I worked hard on that renovation. Stripping, Tearing down, Rebuilding. I was redeeming that house one step at a time.
At first, people sneered. 'You're wasting your time' they said.
But when it was finished and stood beautiful, they recognised the work of art. I guess I was good at restoring houses and decorating them with good things.

God is even better.

Just be who you are.

Leave the rest to God.

> *Let the redeemed of the Lord tell their story.*
> Psalm 107:2 (NIV)

Let God do the wonders. While we stand in awe.

I didn't fully realize it until I began reading the Bible with fresh eyes, but Jesus' ministry was constantly ridiculed by the religious. Jesus was consistently met with opposition - not from outsiders, but from the religious leaders of His day.

The very people who claimed to represent God were the ones most aggressively resisting the move of God in their midst.

The Gospels are full of moments where the Pharisees judged and criticized Jesus. They condemned Him for picking grain on the Sabbath, for not fasting, for eating and drinking with "undesirables."

They ridiculed Him for healing on the Sabbath and scorned Him for ignoring their ceremonial washing traditions. To their law-bound eyes, Jesus could do no right — even as He walked perfectly in the will of God.

> *"Why do you eat and drink with tax collectors and sinners?"*
> they asked (Luke 5:30).

> *"Why are you doing what is unlawful on the Sabbath?"* (Luke 6:2)

"John's disciples often fast and pray, and so do the disciples of the Pharisees, but yours go on eating and drinking." (Luke 5:33) NIV

Even though the list of accusations continued, Jesus did not give in or compromise. Instead, He exposed the hypocrisy behind their rituals. He didn't hold back:

"You pharisees clean the outside of the cup and dish, but inside you are full of greed and wickedness." Luke 11:39 (NIV)

"You give God a tenth of your mint, rue and all other kinds of garden herbs, but you neglect justice and the love of God." Luke 11:42 (NIV)

Tensions build and build until Jesus let them have it, calling them white washed tombs, blind guides, fools and hypocrites. Why? Because they were so obsessed with traditions, rules and outward appearances that they couldn't recognize the very move of God in front of them and the good He was doing.

Jesus came bringing *new wine*, but they clung tightly to their old wineskins. Jesus promoted his new wine all the same.

"And no one pours new wine into old wineskins." Luke 5:37 (NIV)

"And no one after drinking old wine wants the new, for they say, 'The old is better". Luke 5:39 (NIV)

Jesus didn't fit into the religious mould, and the religious representatives of his time hated Him for it. He preached in synagogues to begin with, but soon His ministry spilled outdoors to hillsides, mountaintops, boats, and fields. The synagogues could no longer contain Him, nor did they want to. They tried to quieten him, but Jesus spoke up louder. He wasn't about to limit the calling of God on His life to satisfy human expectations. So, he made bold moves.

Jesus stood firm. He healed the sick, raised the dead, fed the hungry, set captives free. He brought life to dead souls and performed miracles. There were signs and wonders that followed. Evidence that God was with Him and orchestrating the work. Yet the Pharisees, the "representatives of God," were too caught up in hand washing rituals and fasting schedules to acknowledge the lives radically changed through Jesus' ministry. They also failed to see the lack of positive change through their own ministries.

Jesus never measured up to their version of righteousness. But Jesus fulfilled His purpose regardless of their support. And God showed up mightily. The great works of Jesus ministry have been recognised ever since. Passed down for generations, celebrated and taught throughout the ages. Jesus is the central figure of Christianity, the world's largest religion according to Wikipedia.

We don't need to fit into an old wineskin. Or convince religious representatives of our worth. We don't need to earn their approval or waste our lives trying to change their minds about us. If Jesus is our example.

If you've ever been frustrated with church politics, don't criticize the church or the religion - *be* the difference. Don't wait for a church to give you a platform. Jesus didn't ask for one. He *was* the platform, the message. He *was* the move. And He could move anywhere. Sometimes we strive for a little platform in a little church, in a little town, when the bigger platform awaits us (the world) and extends to our friends, family, in-laws, community and workplaces. How can we improve these areas? I can't control the pastor's platform or the musical director at church but I sure can improve the platforms I have been given access to.

I can go where Jesus went-to the non-believers, the outcasts, the open fields? Earth is my playing field. Not just four walls of a church. I can bring positive change everywhere I go. Supported or not. If I'm doing good, who could stop me?

Jesus was ridiculed by the religious but fulfilled his call anyway. He could see the bigger picture and kept creating it. There will always be opposition to great things and resistance to change. You can bring change and great things to earth anyway. You can promote the new wine all the same.

With or without the title.

You may be waiting in life for a title. But life's waiting for you to be the title.

> *For the creation waits in eager expectation for the children of God to be revealed.* Romans 8:19 (NIV)

All Creatures *Great* And Small

If we live in a world where we only accept people that look like us, think like us, and act like us, we will live a very narrow, shallow life. Why should we think we know it all, and our way is the only way?

We are each a piece of a greater puzzle.

The picture is humanity.

We were all designed to fit together beautifully, even though we hold different facets of the ultimate picture, so we don't look, think, or act the same.

Does the fish call out, "We were all made to swim?" Does the caterpillar cry out, "We were all born to transform and take flight?"
Do lions proclaim, "We were created to hunt and rule?"
Do koalas insist, "We were made to climb and feed on eucalyptus?"
Do spiders say, "We are meant to weave webs?"

Each animal is unique.

Each animal is necessary.
They are all part of the animal kingdom, and rightfully so.

Do we ask the fish to conform to a koala's ways?
Would we demand the butterfly crawl like a snake?

Don't we simply receive them as they are?

Jesus accepted everyone.

That's what startled the religious leaders most.
He sat with sinners.
He welcomed outcasts.
He touched the untouchable.
He defended the accused. He advocated for those caught in sin.

The religious leaders wanted to stone those types of people, as their law required. Jesus wanted to help, love, and save them.

Where the law called for punishment,
Jesus offered mercy.
Where others sought distance,
Jesus moved closer.
Loving, healing, restoring.
Even if it meant breaking religious rules.

Like healing on a Sabbath when they said he shouldn't.

Doing good on the Sabbath was more important than a legalistic rule, Jesus highlighted.

Religion…

I know you want to contain me.

I know you want to control me. I know you want me to live a confined, contained life and tell others to do the same. I know you want to bring shame and guilt, judgement, and unworthiness when I don't meet your standards. You want me small and safe, and you want me to keep others small and safe too. But God created me for more.

To think widely.

To live deeply.

To move boldly.

Religious mindsets can't hold me back anymore. Especially when I think of radical Jesus, who flipped tables in the church, preached in open fields (when synagogues had shut him out) was ridiculed by the religious, and was still one hundred percent the Son of God.

> *Don't judge, and you won't be judged.*
> *Don't condemn, and you won't be condemned.*
> *Set free, and you will be set free.*
> Luke 6:37 (WEB)

Hidden *Potential*

When I was in Year 10, I wasn't thriving at school. I used to be academic but that year, striving to be "too cool for school" took over. I stopped doing my homework, skipped some classes and slipped behind.

I had this sense that my teachers didn't like me much, and honestly, I didn't give them much reason to. My grades were terrible.

I remember my English teacher pulling me aside and saying I wouldn't amount to anything. I got a C in his class. That teacher loathed me and my too-cool-for-his-school attitude.

He saw me as a lost cause. I felt it.

Then everything changed.

The next year, my family moved to a new area, a new town, a new school. I had a set of new teachers. A fresh, clean school slate.

Something my new English teacher said to me changed my life. He said to me, before the whole class, "See this girl? She's going to be a writer!"

Wait! What! A writer? Me? My previous teacher didn't think so. Should I mention that?

My new teacher saw something in me no one else had. He saw something I hadn't even seen in myself — a spark, a gift, a voice. The talent to write.

I excelled in English class that year. I guess beliefs are powerful. And so are declarations.

That year, I was ranked first in my year for English, and the following year I earned a HSC score of 91/100.

Not bad for the girl who was once told she would never amount to anything.

What a difference a change made. From the girl at the bottom in Year 10, to the girl coming first in Year 11 and 12. Two very different teachers. Two very different messages. One approach giving me criticism and no hope, the other offering me encouragement and a future.

I bet my second teacher has no idea of the impact he has had on my life. How his belief unlocked hidden potential in me.

Yes, I became a writer, just like he said. And it was his encouragement that opened the door to that self-belief.

I walked into his class thinking I was hopeless at English.
I walked out knowing all things were possible.

He was just doing his job. Showing up.
Teaching. Marking papers. Handing out grades.

Without even knowing it, he impacted my life. Significantly. I've been writing ever since.

One day, I hope I can do the same for someone else.

Speak life and give life. Impact significantly.

For the words of a pessimist have never helped anyone. But a good man's words, benefit many.

> *The words of the godly are a life-giving fountain.*
> Proverbs 10:11 (NLT)

> *A good person's words will benefit many people.*
> Proverbs 10:21 (GNT)

Mr O'Sullivan, this chapter is for you.

> *"For I know the plans I have for you," declares the Lord, "plans to prosper you and not to harm you, plans to give you hope and a future."* Jeremiah 29:11 (NIV)

A *Rug* I Nearly Gave Up On

A long time ago, I purchased an exquisite, woollen rug. I fell in love with it when I was supposed to be shopping for a bathroom vanity. I somehow got distracted by its beauty. The rug ended up coming home with me, as sometimes rugs do.

For the first week, I adored my new woolly rug. It was plush, thick, and comfortable.

But then things changed. It started shedding.

It began to shed all its wool and started making a big woollen mess. What began as a soft haven in the living room quickly became a fluffy nightmare that spread throughout the entire house. The wool attached itself to everything: clothing, bedding, even the meals I was preparing in the kitchen.

My once tidy, fluff-free home was under siege by my new rug. I hated it. What a disaster. What had I done?

The rug left its mark on everything, and everyone — guests included. Experts advised me to groom and vacuum it regularly, promising the shedding would stop after a few months.

But this rug wasn't typical. For some strange reason, my rug was the slow burn that took a lot longer. I seriously considered giving it up.

With patience, persistence, and a whole lot of vacuuming and grooming, the day finally came when the shedding ceased. My home was pristine again. The rug was re-loved. The rug became what I had originally believed it to be — beautiful, functional, worth it. And I was so glad I hadn't given up midway through the process.

I wondered how many woollen rugs had ended up at the dump by a less persistent purchaser. (Wouldn't blame you!)

There needs to be belief in the final product to remain persistent.

If I didn't believe my rug would ever get to a shed-free status, I'm not sure I would have been so loyal to the rug.

But I believed, I persisted, I persevered-and the day came when I celebrated.

Without faith, none of that would have happened

People can be like that rug. Testing our patience, bringing their chaos into our order, and challenging our capacity for grace. Sometimes we're the rug, shedding all over someone else's peace. Sometimes we're the one picking up the fluff. None of us are perfectly put together. None of us are entirely mess-free.

I won't throw judgment if you've given up on a rug or two along your journey. Sometimes there's only so much a person can take and some situations become too heavy to carry. Sometimes, you have to recognize when a 'work in progress' is no longer yours to work on.

Still, I'm thankful we serve a God who doesn't give up on any of us. A God whose love and grace flow equally to the righteous and the unrighteous (Matthew 5:45). God is strong enough to carry anything, even though us humans aren't.

Even when we lose sight of our own potential, God doesn't. God sees the full picture-from beginning to end-and still believes in the masterpiece we're becoming. The worthiness of the finished product.

We were made to be glorious, even when our flaws convince us otherwise.

We are God's children-even with our fluff and disbelief.

We can all be the glorious creations we were created to be.

Because God is the master of redeeming.

Every life holds potential. Belief is the key. Just like this book. If I believe in it enough- and believe you will read it. I will persist in its creation. If I truly believe you will be blessed by the reading of it, I will persist in its promotion and publication. And even though I've got a trunk full of half-finished projects lying dormant from doubt, if I believe in this project enough, I will see it come to fruition.

I don't want to throw out a beautiful rug with potential, just because of the hard work involved in getting it ready. You won't want me to either.

Beliefs have the power to create, make, or break anything. I want my beliefs to back me, not break me.

So, I will endeavour to keep the faith.

To make my beliefs fuel me, not fail me.

All I need is faith.

> *If you have faith as small as a mustard seed, you can say to this mountain, 'Move from here to there,' and it will move. Nothing will be impossible for you.*
> Jesus. Matthew 17:20 (NIV)

Faith

"Your faith has made you well," Jesus once said to a desperate woman in Mark 5:34.

She had suffered for years, weighed down by an illness that no doctor could heal. But she told herself, *"If only I touch Jesus, I will be well."*

She reached out in faith and received exactly what she needed: healing.

Jesus made it clear that it was her *faith* that made her well.

If your faith can make you well,

Then your faith can make you prosperous and successful.

Your faith can make you whole.

Your faith can bring beautiful things into your life.

Your faith can hold your marriage together.

Your faith can carry your career through every storm.

Your faith can strengthen your relationships.

Your faith can unify your family.

Your faith can protect your mental strength and physical health.

But faith fades when you stop believing.

When you lose faith in these things, those things slip away too. You can lose them entirely.

That's why faith matters.
What you believe shapes how you live.

Belief is everything.

Believe in second chances.
Believe in the goodness of God- towards all
Believe in yourself.
Believe in health, in abundance, in true lasting prosperity.
Believe that there is always a way forward-a pathway toward a full life.
Believe in people.
Believe that your body can bounce back.
Believe that your mind can be renewed.
Believe that you can love again and be loved in return.
Believe you are fearfully and wonderfully made.
Believe that your life holds purpose.
Believe you were made in the image of God.

Just believe.

That good things are going to happen. Believe that there's more power in light than in darkness. That good triumphs over evil. That we will have a happy ending.

> *"Be careful how you think; your life is shaped by your thoughts."*
> Proverbs 4:23 (GNT)

God's plans for us are good, but the enemy of our souls tries to plant fear, doubt and worst-case thinking. When we agree with that we partner with the wrong voice and align our thoughts to the wrong purpose. "Fear not" isn't just a command, it's powerful advice. God calls us to trust him and believe for the best.

> *Whatever is true, whatever is noble, whatever is right, whatever is pure, whatever is lovely, whatever is admirable- if anything is excellent or praiseworthy- think about such thing.* Philippians 4:8 (NIV)

So today, I choose to think of the good things.
To dwell on what is beautiful and true.
In me and in everyone around me. I know the news tries to steer me differently. Tells me how bad and hopeless everything is. But I still believe there is more light in this world than darkness. There is more good than evil. There is more hope than despair.

Life is beautiful when you focus on beautiful things.

> *This is the day the Lord has made. We will rejoice and be glad in it.* Psalm 118:24 (NLT)

> *Always be joyful. Never stop praying. Be thankful in all circumstances, for this is God's will for you who belong to Christ Jesus.* 1 Thessalonians 5:16-18 (NLT)

The *Greatest* Reward

Do not throw away your confidence, it will be richly rewarded.
Hebrews 10:35 (NIV)

How often do we abandon our confidence just moments before the reward arrives?

We face setbacks, disappointments, or rejections and we walk away from the life we were trying to create.

We apply for the dream job and hear a "no," so we stop trying altogether, convinced every employer will turn us down too.
We endure a broken relationship, and lose the courage to love again, afraid the pain will simply repeat itself. We pursue a goal, and when it doesn't unfold on our timeline, we decide it wasn't meant to be. Our confidence thrown away.

But what if we didn't throw away our confidence so easily?
What if we were resilient and persistent?
The kind of person who falls a thousand times, but gets up a thousand and one? Believing that one more try was all that was needed?

Most people who succeed in life have faced rejection, failure, criticism, and fierce resistance.
What set them apart was that they continued to believe.

I once heard a story from a former employer about a gathering of green frogs.
They were all racing to climb to the top of a tall pole to claim a prize.
As they climbed, they were heckled by a crowd of bitter, discouraged frogs-ones who had failed the task themselves and now jeered from the sidelines, insisting it couldn't be done.
One by one, the frogs gave up.
Not one succeeded. Until one day, a frog began to climb and didn't stop.
No matter what was shouted at him, he kept going, higher and higher, until he reached the top.

The crowd was stunned.
"How did he do it?" they asked.
When so many others had failed?
The answer was simple.
The frog was deaf.

I think we could all climb higher in life if we became deaf to the negatives, even the ones we tell ourselves-and fix our eyes on the positives.

Maybe we shouldn't be throwing away our confidence so easily,
When it only takes *one* breakthrough to prove it can be done.

I spent years building a library of writing material on my old laptop.
I had worked on my writing diligently for years — pages and pages.

Thousands of words poured out over time, across varying seasons of my life. Like the words in this book. Words on a variety of subjects and topics. It was my life's work. I had no doubt about that.

I had spent countless hours, months, and years writing. Believing the words were too valuable to waste. I had given so much of myself to my writing — time, energy, emotions. I was faithful in recording them. Word for word.

Writing takes time, even when it flows effortlessly.

That laptop was my most prized possession. Not because of the laptop itself, but because of what I had written in it.

If my house had caught fire and no one else was inside, it would have been the first thing I'd seek to save. I probably would have risked my life for it if push had come to shove, like a heroic firefighter.

Nothing else held such irreplaceable value in my material world. It was my dream to one day share my words with the world. Like a gift to give.

My laptop was destroyed along with my first marriage.

I was never able to retrieve it.

Even when a court order demanded it be returned, it never was.

I could have cried at the injustice of it all.

I could have given up, vowed never to write again.

I could have cursed God, man, dreams, and devils.

Instead, I bought a better laptop and wrote a better book.

I told myself: *Nothing will be wasted.*

Those early works were not lost-they were simply the rehearsal for the real performance.

No one sees the practice runs, but they prepare you all the same
You don't need evidence of your practice runs- though they still serve the main event.

Perception was everything in that moment.
It was the difference between carrying on and giving up.
Between being a victim or a victor.

It's not so much about what life throws at you,
But how you handle and process what's been thrown.

I encouraged myself: *A thief never steals invaluable things. They go for the priceless jewels.*

If that was true, then I was even more determined to press on and produce.
Was it easy to write again, knowing all the hours and years I had poured into my previous works brought no reward?
No. It was hard.

I had to push myself hard to get back on the writing horse, doing it either side of a 40-hour working week as a single mother with full time care.

Was it worth it?
You can be the judge of that.
The fruits will speak for themselves.
That's all I can say about that.

Don't throw away your confidence. For it brings with it the greatest of rewards.

> *Reassure the righteous that their good living will pay off.*
> Isaiah 3:10 (MSG)

Undervalued

There was once an experiment conducted by *The Washington Post*. To explore the question:

Would extraordinary people be recognised as extraordinary, if they were placed in an ordinary environment?

To find out, they placed one of the world's greatest violinists in a New York subway station to busk. Dressed in plain clothes, he played the same exquisite, award-winning melodies that had earned him worldwide acclaim. In his hands was a violin worth $3.5 million. Among the thousand people who passed him by, only seven stopped to listen. He played for 45 minutes and collected $32.17 in tips.

Three days earlier, this same violinist had played to a sold-out concert hall, to those who had paid $100 or more per seat for the privilege.

Same musician. Same music. Different setting. We really shouldn't base our worth and value on other people's praise or criticism. If they missed the talent in the subway, they might just miss the greatness in you, too.

Is your environment concealing your greatness? Could it be a case of wrong place, wrong time? Seeds can't grow in all soils. They flourish in the right ones.

An instrument is only as powerful as the hands that play it.
And even when it's played to perfection, some people won't recognize the value in every piece.
Some will ignore it. Some will criticize.
Some won't be capable of seeing brilliance, no matter how clearly you shine.
Some will hate and deliberately bring doubt to your parade, despite your unprecedented value.
Some just don't have it in them to hand out praise.
Sometime people deliberately hurt others in a misguided attempt to ease their own pain.

Motivational speaker Jim Rohn once told a story about a little bird.
The bird sat with his wing covering one eye, softly weeping.
An old owl approached and asked, "Why are you crying?" The little bird pulled his wing away, revealing his eye.
"Oh, I see." The owl said, "You're crying because the big bird pecked out your eye."
"No, said the little bird. "I'm not crying because the big bird pecked out my eyes, I'm crying because I let him."

Don't let anyone destroy your potential, sabotage your purpose, diminish your value, or ever harm you. You are far too precious for that.

> *"If you let people treat you like a doormat, you'll be quite forgotten in the end."* Proverbs 29:21 (MSG)

Greener Grass

When it comes to relationships, they say the grass wouldn't look so green on the other side, if you just watered your own backyard.

But I *did* water my backyard.
For decades.
I remained diligent to its care.
But it still remained dry.
No amount of love, care, or nurture turned it green.
And I wondered why.

The irony was the years spent trying to turn dry grass green, had sucked my green grass dry.

I was withering.
Losing life by the day.

If the soil isn't right, no flower can thrive and grow, no matter how rich its seed.

So, I turned off the tap.
Dropped the hose.
And said farewell to that patch of lifeless grass, riddled with weeds.

Let someone else try to make it flourish.
It couldn't be me.

Now, I water my own grass and it is green everywhere I water it.

I'm rewarded for my efforts.
My landscape is beautiful.
I am diligent over my crop and tend to it well.
And I've learned
when plants blossom,
when life blooms,
tending the garden becomes a joy.

It's easy tending to that type of garden.
It's motivating and rewarding. It heals and gives back. Blesses.
The results of my efforts keep me tending to it.

People admire my garden now.
It is a beautiful sight to behold.
They smell my flowers; they see my roses. They witness the flourish. It
inspires them to garden well, too. It encourages them to pull out their weeds.

My life is mine again,
and it is beautiful.
The contrast is obvious — then to now.

I am glad I was brave, resilient, and courageous enough to no longer be captive to dry grass. It wasn't easy.

I walked a hard road, but my values and faith supported it.

Those that come into my life now only add value.
Those that don't aren't given a seat at my table.
I'd rather a humble table with peace, than a grand one filled with strife.
I'm surrounded with love, kindness, and good people.

It was never about the waterer.
It was always about the grass.

> *A good tree produces good fruit, and a bad tree produces bad fruit. A good tree can't produce bad fruit, and a bad tree can't produce good fruit.* Matthew 7:17-18 (NLT)

Some trees simply no longer deserve your watering hose.

I'm glad I chose me.
Even though I lost a grand house and a lifetime of accumulated possessions in the process.
I would choose me again-if faced with the same path, and the same set of circumstances.

I'm proud of the life I'm creating.
I'm doing more than just fine.

Sometimes, the grass *is* actually greener on the other side.

This is my side of the story anyway.

Life's too short to be tied to unhappy strife filled, misaligned unions. If you must, set yourself free.

> *Do two people walk hand in hand if they aren't going to the same place?* Amos 3:3 (MSG)

The *Rebuild*

We grow up with a dream of forever. Of white dresses, golden rings and unshakable love. We walk down the aisle and declare, *"For better or worse, till death do us part."*

We cleave to our partner like the Bible tells us to do in Genesis 2:24. With full hearts and hopeful eyes, we commit. The happily ever after begins like a promise written in stone.

When lived according to God's heart, marriage is a gift — holy, enduring, powerful. It's the ideal, and when it works, it's beautiful. It serves us, our families, and society exceptionally well. In a perfect world, it's the best practice model for all parties involved.

Science even supports the notion that love and partnership is a powerful thing. It can lower your blood pressure, strengthen the immune system, combat depression, and increase longevity. The benefits of love and partnership, both emotional and physical are undeniable. When we find a heart that sees us - really sees us - and chooses us daily, we carry something rare and divine. An inner knowing that we are not alone. Someone has chosen to journey with us.

A marriage covenant is one of the most powerful and sacred unions on earth. It represents a lifelong promise between two people to love, support and remain faithful to each other. We're naturally wired to yearn for this level of connection and commitment. We want it. We long for it. We all deserve it because, deep down, we were designed for it. Life feels lacking without it. Two hearts are better than one.

No one says their wedding vows planning for a breakdown. No bride thinks of court dates while walking down the aisle. No groom imagines custody papers as he slips on a ring. We all begin with hope, with love, and the very best intentions. And yet sometimes, even with sincerity and effort, things fall apart. Sometimes, despite prayer, commitment, and faith, the road ends and people must part. That doesn't mean the covenant was meaningless. It means we live in a world where people are fallible, broken and in need of grace. Yes, most relationships should be fought for and not all seasons are going to feel like love. But others become unsafe, unrecognizable and damaging.

When that happens, God's mercy doesn't leave us.

> *The Lord is close to the brokenhearted; he rescues those whose spirits are crushed.* Psalm 34:18 (NLT)

Sometimes, in a broken world, people reach the end of what they can carry. And in those moments, God's grace doesn't run out, it runs in.

There is healing after heartbreak.
There is redemption after rupture.
There is life - good, beautiful life - even when the last chapter ended differently than we originally intended.

Because God doesn't measure our worth by our marital status. God measures it by his love for us — unchanging, unshakable, eternal.

What if, when possible, we choose to honour the good that was shared. To speak grace instead of venom. What if we modeled that for our children? To walk away with dignity instead of destruction. To choose peace as we part. That kind of ending may not be the fairytale we imagined, but it could still be an ending full of wisdom, grace and strength.

Of course, not all relationships are healthy, and not everyone deserves a glowing report.
But if you can find even one good thing to take out of the experience, focus on that.
For your soul's sake.
Because bitterness won't build your future. But gratitude will.

We often think the most important thing to protect in divorce is our wealth.
The house, the car, the material possessions.
If you ever walk through divorce, the lawyers will confirm it.
They'll tell you: "Protect your assets, secure your entitlements."
And I'm not saying you shouldn't.
But let me offer this deeper truth:
Your greatest asset is *you*.

Protect your vessel. Guard your heart.
Shield it from bitterness, hate, envy, stress, greed, and revenge.
Keep it soft. Keep it kind. Keep it loving.
Because no matter how fierce the storm of divorce and separation can get, if you protect *you*, you will rise again.

Every. Single. Time.

Don't worry about the hair — mine was falling out from stress.

Don't worry about the weight — mine was dropping rapidly from worry.

Don't worry about the wealth — mine was tangled in lawyers and property settlement delays.

Don't worry about the car — mine wasn't even in my name and I was unknowingly driving it around unregistered for weeks.

Don't worry about the job, the shares, the super, the status.

Yes, those things matter… somewhat.

But most of all, *how are you?*

How is your heart?

Because *out of it will flow the issues of life.*

> *Guard your heart above all else, for it determines the course of your life.* Proverbs 4:23 (NLT)

If your heart is steady, don't fret so much about your bank balance, your waistline, or the texture of your skin.

If your heart is full of peace, love, joy, and patience, what could possibly unravel you?

If you tend to your heart, the rest will follow:

The weight will rise or fall as it should.

The right partner will appear.

Your quality of life will improve.

Friends will surround you.

Opportunities will find you.

Healing will come.

If the heart is whole, life will flow.

If the heart is hard, even the strongest house will crack. I'm sure you have heard the saying *"Ships don't sink because of the water around them, but from the water that gets in them."*

That is why it was never my goal to hate or avenge when my marriage crumbled. It was to heal and be whole.

I didn't want to match the mess; I wanted to protect my peace.

And my future self is grateful for that decision.

I could have spent the rest of my lifetime, telling a tale of hardship, injustice, and betrayal.

But instead, I chose healing.

I chose to rise.

I chose to rebuild.

I turned the page and held onto the version of me I most wanted to be: a sweetheart.

I refused to let divorce, pain, or nasty people, turn me into someone I'm not.

I committed to *better* and kept my faith. I forgave misguided judgements and developed strength and resilience.

Judge me not unless you've walked a mile in my shoes.

Judge him not unless you've done the same.

There doesn't always have to be a villain in every story.

And I refuse to be the victim.

We are all deeply loved by God.

Whether married, single, or divorced.

Whether the instigator of divorce or the recipient.

We came into this world alone.

We will leave it alone.

Our eternal connection is to God, not a spouse.

We are God's — loved, seen, and valued.

Whether our marriage made it or not.

We are loved. Always and eternally.

People are drawn to light.

To warmth.

To positive energy.

So protect yours.

If you want to attract beauty into your next season, watch your words. Guard your energy. Train your lips to speak life, hope, healing, and abundance.

Because as Proverbs 18:21 reminds us:

> *"The tongue can bring death or life."* (NLT)

So, speak life.

Prophesy peace.

Declare blessing.

Take action toward the life you've dreamed of.

Your future isn't found in your past.

It's shaped by your present words and daily steps.

If your heart remains soft, still open, still alive to love, to hope and to Gods blessings, then you haven't lost everything. You've kept the most important part of you intact.

And from there... you can rebuild anything.

For though the righteous fall seven times, they rise again.
Proverbs 24:16 (NIV)

Love is patient and kind. Love is not jealous or boastful or proud or rude. It does not demand its own way. It is not irritable, and it keeps no record of being wronged. It does not rejoice about injustice but rejoices whenever the truth wins out.
1 Corinthians 13:4 (NLT)

The Everyday *Heroes*

We were in a room filled to the brim with little people — babies, toddlers, and preschoolers. All gathered to watch a popular traveling kids' show.

To say it was hectic would be an understatement. It was chaotic, overwhelming, and loud. Very loud!

The room was a tapestry of different ages and stages. Some babies were screaming; some were calm and content. Some were tired and touchy; others were cheerful. Some children whined and wriggled with restlessness, while others sang along with joy, relishing the moment. A few anxiously clung to their mothers. Some threw tantrums, while others sat shy and sheepish not daring to rock the boat. Every child is unique, with their own set of character traits and personalities.

I was sitting pretty that day, my one and only four-year-old at the time, nestled in my lap happily munching on snacks and enjoying the show. I wasn't juggling multiple children with varying needs. I wasn't praying for my child to stop being dramatic and start being calm. I wasn't flustered or trying to manage a strong-willed child mid-meltdown. For once, everything was aligned. The sun, moon, and stars, but I wasn't fooled into thinking I'd never been there in the chaos of parenting.

Oh, I had. For years.

Years of enduring the tantrums at public functions, of having to leave events early, of outbursts and interruptions. Years of sacrifice and public humiliation. Of sleepless nights with a colicky reflux baby. With age, my daughter was calmer and wiser, though we still had our moments.

That day, as I looked around the chaotic room, I noticed something else: the mothers, the parents. The carriers of those little loads. And I thought: *What an army.* An army of warriors. True heroes of society. Our everyday heroes.

I witnessed that day the often unseen force of child-raisers. Those pouring love and wisdom into the next generation. Sacrificing their lives for the ones they love more than life itself.

The work is constant. Grueling. Draining. Often unrewarded.

Of all the years I spent in the corporate world, no job ever came close to the challenge of motherhood. In the corporate world I had uninterrupted tea breaks. I could reset when I needed to, plan my days, take sick or annual leave. My daily task list was a fraction of the one I faced as a mother, and it didn't come with defiance, resistance, tears — or a toddler demanding to go pantless to the shops. It requires a delicate skill-set and a strength of steel to raise children — qualities I'm still working on, as each year brings its own new set of challenges and skills.

I remember those early years. The constant, relentless grind. Even just getting out of the door those days felt like a major achievement. They may look little but trust me, children are a force to be reckoned with.

And then there's all the pressure modern parents face.

"Have they reached their milestones? Are they toilet trained? Eating solids? Walking yet? Talking? Have they given up the dummy? Should they have even had it in the first place?" The list is endless. Troubling. Worrying. We could drive ourselves crazy trying to do it perfectly. We do it all for love, what else is the motive?

The early childhood season has passed for me now, the nappies, the sleepless nights. But I won't forget its challenges or the joy it brought. Motherhood is precious but it's not all lullabies and chubby cheeks. Sometimes it's bone-deep exhaustion. It's crying in the bathroom because you haven't had a moment to breathe. It's feeding someone else before you remember to eat. It's holding a screaming baby with one arm and trying to hold your sanity with the other. It's a kind of work no one sees, an invisible labour of love. Those thousand tiny sacrifices that don't make it into the baby books-heaven notices and keeps score of.

So, here's to the mothers, fathers, and care takers. Doing the impossible with tired eyes and unwavering devotion.

If you haven't heard it recently: Thank you.

Thank you for all that you do.

I know it's exhausting and, at times, thankless. I know it requires sacrifice, patience, and grace. I know it disrupts your finances and steals your downtime. You juggle food prep, nappy changes, sleepless nights, and all the other mammoth tasks that come with the job. The laundry is overflowing, the house a mess. Your body is put on the line often battling exhaustion, and a host of other physical and emotional challenges that come with the territory.

Only heroes walk this road. Only heroes could.

Sooner or later, you'll look back and reminisce about the way you could scoop your child into your arms, carry them around, and see their smile, pure and untainted by the world. You'll miss the influence you once had, when their world starts expanding to others. Before you know it, they leave your nest. They fly into the world, they become you — an adult. You played your part. You raised your child. You did good. They mimic you either way.

One day our children will have their turn to raise a generation of tomorrow's citizens, and maybe then, they'll look back and recognize us for what we were:
Everyday heroes.

Unsung but indispensable. Invaluable to their upbringing.

That's who we are and why we're here.

> *Your greatest contribution to the world may not be something you do, but someone you raise.* Andy Stanley

> *Direct your children onto the right path, and when they are older, they will not leave it.* Proverbs 22:6 (NLT)

We are doing our best with the hearts we've been given to raise, but from the very beginning our children have belonged to God. God has just entrusted them to us for this moment. So when the weight feels too heavy, when worry creeps in, or when they walk through valleys we cannot fix, we remember, God holds them closer than we ever could. Their lives, their stories and their futures rest in hands far surer than ours. And ultimately their eternity is not anchored in this world, but in the promise of forever with God.

> *"Before I formed you in the womb, I knew you. Before you were born, I set you apart for my holy purpose."*
> Jeremiah 1:5 (MSG)

The *Benefits* Of Vinegar

I was knee-deep in the trenches of toddler tantrums, blatant defiance, and public meltdowns. Every single day, every minute, felt like a challenge. I quickly realised some kids are naturally compliant, quietly following the leader. Mine wasn't one of them. If I said "right," she went left. If I said "up," she went down. If I said "stop," she kept going. Challenge, challenge, challenge —that was the motto of those days. Nothing was easy. Nothing ran smoothly. Just getting out of the door on time, dressed and somewhat intact felt like a monumental achievement in those days. She was the toddler that went to princess parties dressed up as a rowdy cowgirl. She acted like it too. Unique, outstanding, full of life and spark, but exhausting to raise. She didn't follow the rules. None of the expert parenting advice worked. I became tired trying.

I know a strong will, endless energy, and a gutsy spirit are qualities to be admired. But when those qualities are packed into a three-year-old's body, you get a recipe for chaos and mayhem. Add sleepless nights, no respite, and a mountain of responsibilities for mum, and you've got yourself a short fuse.

It had been one meltdown after another that day; one humiliating exit after another from every child-focused event we'd attended. I'd been spat at, kicked, and screamed at. I'd had my hair pulled, my face slapped and spent my day navigating child politics and negotiating toy ownership, all to little effect. My patience was on the edge.

I gathered the last shreds of my pride and headed home. Who needs a gold star from the Parent Committee of the World's Most Perfect Parents anyway? I was used to their disapproving frowns and critiques. Besides, I wasn't trying to win Parent of the Year. I was just trying to survive that year.

I arrived home frazzled and disheartened, wondering when, oh when, I would see the light at the end of the tunnel? I loved my daughter more than anything in the world, but why was she so difficult? I voiced this to God.

I poured myself my umpteenth cup of coffee and began to ponder the deep mystery that I had been given the honour to raise her. That's when it happened. Miss Three, the self-appointed expert on everything, spotted a clear bottle of vinegar in the pantry and demanded water.

"That's not water, it's vinegar. I'll get you some water," I said, grabbing a cup of water and putting it in front of her.

"No, that one!" she pointed, her finger zeroing in on the vinegar bottle.

"Sweetheart, it's vinegar, not water. Here, have your water."

"Noooo! That water!" she screamed, her face contorted with fury. Her body arching back. And then the battle began: scream, demand, scream, demand. She wasn't letting up.

It was the final straw. The moment when the whole day's madness came to a head.

So, I did what any self-respecting, well-educated parent would do in that moment... I gave her a sip of her water, also known as vinegar.

The tantrum stopped immediately. My little girl, so proud and defiant, pretended she'd sipped nothing more than water. Not even a flinch, not a blink. She acted like nothing had happened. And in her mind, she was right, and I was wrong, once again.

She never asked me for "vinegar water" again though.

Was it wrong? Was it right?

We're all doing our best in the wild, wonderful, and often wearying land of parenting. Some days we feel like champions; other days we're riddled with guilt. I've had my share of not-so-proud mothering moments — ones I wouldn't exactly frame on the wall but they happened all the same.

One such moment just happened to involve vinegar. Since then, I've come to learn the proven benefits of vinegar. How it lowers cholesterol, helps regulate blood sugar and aids digestion. I also discovered its unexpected power to humble a very determined three-year-old.

> *We know that in all things God works for good with those who love him.* Romans 9:28 (GNT)

If you're struggling in this sacred, exhausting, beautiful work of raising children — chin up. The hard moments don't last forever. The tantrums fade, the challenges shift, and in time, you'll look back and see how far you've come.

My daughter grew. She evolved. And now, the traits that once caused worry and concern, have become the very qualities that make her shine and stand out in a crowd.

I learned something essential from my toddler parenting days: our children aren't blank slates handed to us to mould into our ideal image. They come with a slate already painted. With their own souls, their own quirks and strengths, their own callings and natures. Our job isn't to perfect them, but to nurture them — to hold space for who they already are and who they are becoming. We don't always get it right but the greatest gifts we can offer are grace, understanding and unconditional love. Everything else flows from there.

God's masterpiece in each of us is still unfolding, and the little ones are just on their first brushstrokes.

> *He has made everything beautiful in its time.*
> Ecclesiastes 3:11 (NIV)

The Bible's *Blessings*

— ❧ —

With over 5 billion copies sold, around 100 million more printed each year, written across 1,500 years by 40 different authors, and translated into nearly 900 languages, the Bible is a phenomenon. Even if you don't read it or believe it. There is no other book that has sustained such momentum through the centuries. It has *thrived* and *survived*. Shaped cultures, inspired movements and endured for thousands of years.

I read the Bible a lot. It does good to my soul.

And yet, I've often wondered how can one person can read the Bible and be stirred toward love, peace and compassion while another reads it and justifies violence, exclusion or hate?

The answer is not in the Bible itself, but in the heart of the reader.

The Bible is God-breathed, consistent and trustworthy. But people have long twisted its words to serve their own agendas. It's not the fault of the text, but it's the misuse of it that causes harm.

To the racist, Scripture becomes a weapon.
To the unmerciful, it becomes a justification.

To the narcissist, it becomes a tool for control.
To the hateful, a shield for hate.

For those who come with humility and love, Scripture is life giving — a call to forgive, to serve, to heal, and to love.

The way we handle Scripture matters. The same verse quoted out of context can build or destroy. Without wisdom, context, and the spirit of God, truth can be twisted.

Yes it's possible to find verses that appear to contradict each other. One passage warns to abstain from wine: another shows Jesus turning water into it. One speaks of women being silent; another describes Deborah leading an army of men.

The Bible is layered, deep, and complex. It takes years to study, and even then, it cannot be fully understood — not even by the greatest scholar.

The devil used Scripture when tempting Jesus in the wilderness.
The devil quoted, *"He will command His angels concerning you,"* (Matthew 4:6), tempting Jesus to test God and throw Himself onto rocks.
Jesus responded with more Scripture, rightly applied in wisdom, truth and the correct spirit, *"It is also written…"*

Yes, you can do that. Interpret Scripture with Scripture.

The Bible is susceptible to being misused when removed from its context or wielded without love.

Not everyone who sits at a piano can play Beethoven.
Some create soul-stirring beauty, and we will all enjoy their music.
Others will create chaos and make a mess with those keys.
The piano didn't change. The player did. Did the creator of the piano intend for the latter in the original design? Of course not.

The Apostle Paul was once targeting Christians with zeal, believing he was obeying scripture. But when he encountered Jesus, his entire understanding was transformed. The same man who once used scripture as a weapon become one of its greatest messengers of love and grace.

It's not surprising that from one Bible emerged many different churches, doctrines, and denominations.

Some churches only let men lead.
Others have women at the helm.
Some prohibit leaders from marrying.
Others won't let you lead unless you're married.
Some embrace all people.
Others exclude certain types.
Some serve wine at communion.
Others ban alcohol altogether.

Each group finds biblical support for their convictions.

I don't believe Scripture is confused, but I do believe people are diverse.
God gave us free will.
And we'll find whatever we go looking for.

Mother Teresa read the Bible and blessed the world. Yet the same text has sometimes been twisted by others to justify war, oppression and unimaginable evils.

How we use it matters. Will we bash or bless? Condemn or redeem? Wound or heal

We have the power to use everything in life for good or evil.
Our money, our resources, our time, our thoughts, our words… and yes, our Bibles.

As for me-
I want to use the Scriptures and benefit mankind.
Because I've found life, hope, and truth in the Bible's pages.

That's the song I'm singing today, inspired by scripture. Songs of love and grace.

If God is love, shouldn't His followers be the same?

Love is not a replacement for truth, but it's the lens through which all Scripture is to be understood.

> *"So now I am giving you a new commandment: Love each other. Just as I have loved you, you should love each other. Your love for one another will prove to the world that you are my disciples."* John 13:34 (NLT)

The *Builders*

I knew a boy in his youth. Popular, good-looking, and full of charm.

He partied hard, took drugs, travelled, and hooked up with countless women.

He was living for the moment, loving his life.

While others were working hard and investing in their futures, he was chasing cheap thrills.

While his peers got married and began to build steady lives, he was living it up in true party-boy style.

Life eventually caught up with him. His looks could no longer carry him. The years had taken their toll. He had nothing to show for his life thus far.

The builders settled down to enjoy the fruits of their labour.

There were no fruits of long-term partying to enjoy.

I saw the regret in his eyes, as he realised his folly. The quiet desperation of someone who knew what they'd squandered.

Was it too late to start what should have started long ago?

He was older now, midway through his life, relying on elderly parents for shelter.

The builders had homes of their own. To raise their children, love their wife's and relish the blessings.

He had none of these things.

The party lifestyle had fooled him. Reality had humbled.

It's wiser to be a builder.

The children rise up and call the builders blessed.

> *God-loyal people, living honest lives, make it much easier for their children.* Proverbs 20:7 (MSG)

> *If you live upright and well, you get the credit.* Ezekiel 18:20 (MSG)

> *God's paths get you where you want to go. Right-living people walk them easily; wrong living people are always tripping and stumbling.* Hosea 14:9 (MSG)

The *Gambler*

If you gamble, you most likely will be broke.
Not instantly. It's a slow drain — quiet, constant, cunning.

People refuse to give ten percent of their wage to the church
But will feed twenty to the poker machines without question.
You don't *have* to do either…
But if you gamble, you most likely *will* be broke.

Do you think these machines are designed to lose?
That the clubs installed them to make their patrons blessed and prosperous?

That would be a dumb design for a business trying to profit.

Look around.
The clubs look grand — renovated, glittering, thriving.
But the gamblers?
Not so good.

Ask yourself: *Who's really winning?*

I'd rather feed a soul than a soulless machine.

But that's just me.

A man once asked me for five dollars.
I thought he was struggling to eat, so I gave it to him.
He walked straight into the club.
To feed his addiction.
I guess he *was* struggling.
Struggling with an addiction to a machine.
A machine offering false hope. A machine making him poor.
A machine taking more than it will ever give.

Sometimes we keep returning to the very thing that empties us, expecting a different outcome. The man came out and needed five more.

I said a silent prayer. Gambling your money is one thing.
But don't gamble your life. Put your trust in God.
The only One who never takes from you to bless you.

> *Change your life, not just your clothes. Come back to God, your God. And here's why: God is kind and merciful. He takes a deep breath, puts up with a lot. This most patient God, extravagant in love, always ready to cancel catastrophe. Who knows? Maybe he'll do it now, maybe he'll turn around and show pity. Maybe, when all's said and done, they'll be blessings full and robust for your God!* Joel 2:13-14 (MSG)

The Worrier

I used to live ahead of myself-
Projecting fears and hopes into a future not yet born.
My mind spun tales of next week,
next month,
next year.
Always somewhere else,
but never fully in each moment.

Chasing unfinished lists,
imagining outcomes,
solving problems that didn't yet exist.

It was exhausting.

But now,
I've learned to confine my worries to today alone.
Just today.
Have I done what is mine to do now?
If so, then I can rest.
To carry the burden of tomorrow
is to misuse the energy reserved for today.

*"Don't worry about tomorrow, for tomorrow will bring its
own worries. Today's trouble is enough for today."*
Matthew 6:34 (NLT)

The ancient wisdom still holds true.

So, these days, when I wake
and my mind races ahead-
to Christmas (Six months away)
to how I'll ever retire (30 years away)
or how my daughter will own a home someday.

I pause.
I tell my heart and mind
That's tomorrow's work.
Today has its own assignments. Stay focused on today

This practice, this daily reining in-
it doesn't come easily.
But oh, what peace it will bring.

One day at a time.
One breath at a time.
One task at a time.

There's a stillness in trusting
that I am not alone in this.

*You will keep in perfect peace all who trust in you, all whose
thoughts are fixed on you!* Isaiah 26:3 (NLT)

"So do not be afraid, little flock. For it gives your Father great happiness to give you the Kingdom." Luke 12:32 (NLT)

So let today be enough.
Let grace meet you here.
And let tomorrow wait
in the hands of God.

Who will never leave nor forsake you. Who has told you to "fear not"

Don't fret or worry. Instead of worrying, pray. Let petitions and praises shape your worries into prayers, letting God know your concerns. Before you know it, a sense of God's wholeness, everything coming together for good, will come and settle you down. It's wonderful what happens when Christ displaces worry at the center of your life. Summing it all up, friends, I'd say you'll do best by filling your minds and meditating on things true, noble, reputable, authentic, compelling, gracious—the best, not the worst; the beautiful, not the ugly; things to praise, not things to curse. Put this into practice what you learned from me, what you heard and saw and realized. Do that, and God, who makes everything work together, will work you into his most excellent harmonies. Philippians 4:6-9 (MSG)

Celebrations Of *Life*

"Better to spend your time at funerals than at parties. After all, everyone dies—so the living should take this to heart. Sorrow is better than laughter, for sadness has a refining influence on us. A wise person thinks a lot about death, while a fool thinks only about having a good time." Ecclesiastes 7:2-3 (NLT)

I went to a funeral today.
Celebrating a man who had lived a very good life.
The room was full of people who could testify to this.
A testimony to the kind of man he was.

I can see why the Bible says spending time at funerals is more valuable than spending time at parties. Parties are fun but funerals have a refining influence on us. They keep us grounded. They remind us we're mortal. They refine us. They make us reflect.

It would be nice to reach the end of our mortal life knowing we had lived a life we could be proud of. To have a room full of people sharing stories that honoured our choices and our character.

I have witnessed a man who didn't live such a good life, screaming in fear on his way out. It put the fear of God and hell in everyone who heard. Including me.

If one day we must give an account of our life to God,
it would be nice to have a good account.
Like retiring with a strong superannuation fund-
the relief, knowing the rest of your days are taken care of.

> *"His master replied, 'Good job! You're a good and faithful servant! You proved that you could be trusted with a small amount. I will put you in charge of a large amount. Come and share your master's happiness."* Matthew 25:23 (GW)

Maybe this earth is the "little" we're entrusted with-
and eternity, the "large."

Come on in and share My happiness?
Yes, please.

When was the last time you felt truly happy?
Vibrantly, soul-deep, full of joy, happy.

Earth has its trials, pains, and struggles.
Eternity holds the treasures and rewards for them.

We are spirit — eternal — having a temporary earthly experience.
Our bodies may wear out, but our spirits live on when fragile bodies can no longer house them.
We don't know when our time will come.

None of us do. That day cannot be predicted, although it's the earthly guarantee.

So, I want to make the most of now.
Since tomorrow isn't promised.
Eddie Jaku wrote in his book- 'The happiest man on earth'
"Tomorrow will come—but first, enjoy today."
I like that.
But sometimes?
Tomorrow doesn't come.
Even more incentive to enjoy today.

We all can be wonderful humans and impact life in such a way that people will speak well of us at our funerals.

Were we perfect? No.
Were we worthy? Maybe not.
Did we make a difference? Yes, we did. Sometimes for the better, sometimes for the worse. Intentionally and unintentionally.
Are we loved by God? Yes, we are.
Absolutely, yes, we all are.

If we mess this up, do we get another chance to come here again, and improve our game?

Don't tell me I'm not loved by God because I went through divorce.
Don't tell me I'm not loved by God because I don't make it to church every Sunday or sing in the choir like I used to.
Don't tell them they're unloved because they're living differently to you.
Don't shame them.

Love them.
That's what Jesus would do.

> *Won't he leave the ninety-nine others on the hills to go out to search for the one that is lost. And if He finds it, I tell you the truth, He will rejoice over it more than over the ninety-nine who didn't wander away!* Matthew 18:12-13 (NLT)

That's good to know, isn't it? The Good Shepherd will find us and rejoice. Not condemn us, not shame us, not weigh in on our guilt. Rejoice!

I was here.
I cried.
I loved.
I tried.
I persevered.
I got knocked down and got back up again.
I had joy.
I had sorrow.
I sinned.
I received grace.
I was loved - and I loved deeply.
I was surrounded by beautiful people with beautiful souls.
And I encountered some broken souls too.
I tried my best to be one of the beautiful ones.
I gave it my best shot.
Where I failed, *grace stepped in.*

We are all saved by grace.
Thank God for that.

"I have fought the good fight. I have finished the race, and I have remained faithful. And now the prize awaits me- the crown of righteousness, which the Lord, the righteous Judge, will give to me on the day of his return. And the prize is not just for me but for all who eagerly look forward to his appearing." 2 Timothy 4:7-8 (NLT)

Life, lovely while it lasts, is soon over. Life as we know it, precious and beautiful, ends. The body is put back in the same ground it came from. The spirit returns to God, who first breathed it. Ecclesiastes 12:6-7 (MSG)

A *Note* from the Author

I was told the average book should be at least 40,000 words. Since my book and I are quite happy being ordinary- I stopped a little short of that.

My book and I don't feel lacking.
Even if we should.

Since *you* are my audience, I thought, maybe you would prefer a shorter read anyhow.
A read that gets to the point quicker. One that you can read repeatedly without being too overwhelming or demanding too much of your precious time. I know how busy life can be. With our schedules and life's demands. So, I politely took one moment of your time. Nothing more, nothing less. I was sure you wouldn't mind.

I'm grateful for this moment. The moment you have taken to read this book and read my thoughts. They are my own, though they may evolve with time. In fact, I hope they do. I can save that for book two. "A picture and a thousand words evolved"
My heart hopes you have been blessed by these words. Words really can change a person or a nation if given the chance. They can bless and uplift. Heal and give hope. Words are powerful. If you believe the Bible, God created the world with His.

It only takes a spark, remember, to set off a forest fire. A careless or wrongly placed word out of your mouth can do that. By our speech we can ruin the world, turn harmony to chaos, throw mud on a reputation, send the world up in smoke and go up in smoke with it, smoke right from the pit of hell. This is scary: You can tame a tiger, but you can't tame a tongue —it's never been done. The tongue runs wild, a wanton killer. With our tongues we bless God our Father; with the same tongue we curse the very men and women he made in his image. Curses and blessings out of the same mouth! My friends, this can't go on. A spring doesn't gush fresh water one day and brackish the next, does it? Apple trees don't bear strawberries, do they? Raspberry bushes don't bear apples, do they? You're not going to dip into a polluted mud hole and get a cup of clear, cool water, are you? James 3:5-12 (MSG)

Thank you again for letting me share my thoughts, my heart, and some of my journey with you. I hope it felt like drinking a clear, cool, refreshing cup of water, on a hot day when your soul was parched.

It started with a picture and a thousand words —
Then I added thirty-two thousand more.

With love,

Kellie

....●

For further engagement with the author, you are welcome to connect or reach out via:
Instagram: @kelliehutchinson_writer
Email: kelliehutchinsonwriter@gmail.com